TUTORING

Philip Waterhouse

Network Educational Press

Network Educational Press Ltd
PO Box 635
Stafford
ST17 OJR

First Published 1991
© Copyright Network Educational Press Ltd

ISBN 1 85539 006 X

Printed and bound in Trowbridge, Great Britain by Redwood Books.

Contents

INTRODUCTION

There is a great revival of interest in student-centred systems of education. Much of it is attributable to government initiatives such as TVEI, CPVE, the GCSE, and the National Curriculum. But these initiatives were only reflecting the concerns and ambitions that were already in existence within the teaching profession. In secondary education the sixties and seventies witnessed a number of developments in *Resource-based Learning*, and this was followed in the eighties by project development in *Supported Self-Study*, which led to the Training Agency- now called the Training and Enterprise Education Directorate (TEED) - to launch its initiative in *Flexible Learning*. Within adult education and further education the same period has been marked by developments in *Open Learning*.

All these initiatives share the same broad student-centred philosophy, although each has contributed its own special emphasis.

- ☐ *Resource-based Learning* emphasised the need for the student to have access to information and ideas directly through the resources without necessarily having to rely on the teacher's mediation. The initiative promoted the skills of finding, retrieving and using information - the information skills.

- ☐ *Supported Self-Study* emphasised the need for young students to have support from the teacher in their progress towards independence in learning.

- ☐ *Flexible Learning* emphasised the wide range of possible resources and situations and the learner taking greater responsibility for his/her own learning.

- ☐ *Open Learning* emphasised the freedom of the learner to have access to learning and to determine when, where, and how the learning should take place. It was designed for the adult sector, but the ideas have been used in both further and secondary education.

While the differences are interesting and of some significance, it is fair to say that these movements have more similarities than differences. In this book we are not attempting to differentiate between the systems. We are simply concerned with the teacher's desire to help learners to become more independent, by giving them support and leading them towards the practice of greater responsibility.

There has been a long history of attempts to individualise education and to make the learning process more student-centred. On the whole results have been disappointing. Teachers have often found that the conditions under which they work in our schools are not really conducive to these tailor-made arrangements. They identify two main problems.

1) Time. The teacher's time always seems to be in such short supply. The underlying causes are the student-teacher ratio and the rapidly growing demands on the teachers and the schools. Teachers are constantly trying to find ways of overcoming the acute shortage of time. They become experts in compromises - getting some kind of result even though it falls short of the ideal. It is no wonder that teaching is so often organised round the teacher, not round the students.

2) Resources. Although public expenditure on education is increasing much work is done with only subsistence level resources. This state of affairs encourages unambitious planning and a preference for the cheapest method of delivery.

These two problems are sufficiently large to suggest that the attempts to make learning more student-centred are severely handicapped at the outset. And there is little that the teachers can do to improve matters.

On the other hand it can be argued that some of the attempts at student-centred learning have run into difficulties that are more attributable to technical mistakes made in the classroom than to the background environment. In other words there are some things that the teachers can themselves do to help bring about the desired changes. These are the main technical mistakes which have been made in the classroom.

The belief in instant autonomy for the student

In a rush of enthusiasm many have made the mistake of demanding too much of their students too quickly. From an existing position of dependence the students have suddenly been catapulted into a new complex world of choices, decision making, and organisation. Not surprisingly they have run into difficulties.

The belief that to be student-centred the work must be organised individually

The argument went as follows. All the students are different one from another. Therefore they need individual programmes of study and should be allowed to work at their own pace. This is logical enough and teachers certainly need to think through the implications of individual differences and individual needs. But it is not wise to set up a system dedicated to individual working. Students do not thrive when working exclusively in isolation. Most of them need to spend a high proportion of their time working with their fellow students.

The belief that student-centred learning requires specially designed learning materials

This emphasised the materials so much that there was an implication that the teacher was not so important! This downgrading of the role of the teacher was a serious misjudgement. If students are to develop a sense of greater responsibility for their own learning they need all the help and guidance that the teacher can give. They can only demonstrate their developing sense of responsibility through personal contact - explaining what they have done, justifying their decisions and actions, and displaying their mastery of the new learning. So in student-centred learning the teacher's role is *more* important, not less.

The belief that student-centred learning should be more permissive and less structured than didactic teaching

Letting them make their own decisions about *what* they do and *when* and *where* and *how* they work seems a friendly and warm approach to teaching. It is all too easy to let this slip so that the students' own self-will becomes the most important thing. But life is not like that and students should not be encouraged to think that way. Guidance in student-centred learning should be much more in tune with real life; it encourages the student to think and act in responsible and mature ways.

The belief that the new systems should lead to the abandonment of traditional class teaching

The criticisms of class teaching have been overdone, and the student-centred systems are sometimes oversold. Students need to experience a broad repertoire of teaching and learning styles.

> Throughout these developments in the seventies and eighties one idea emerged that has become central to thinking about student-centred learning. This was the crucial importance of the guidance and support and management which is provided by the teacher.

- In the developments of resource-based learning the term *classroom management* was coined to express the importance attached to the way that the teacher supported students who were learning directly from resources in classrooms and libraries.

- In the subsequent developments in supported self-study, the original belief in the power of carefully prepared materials for self-study by students of minority subjects was soon replaced by an emphasis on the support of the teacher, and an extension of the idea into the mainstream of the curriculum.

- In the Open Learning movement the vague idea of guidance as an optional extra for students who were working independently of the normal classes was replaced by a recognition that the teacher's guidance was crucial.

We have now reached a point where the role of the teacher in guidance, support and management is almost universally recognised. The term *tutoring* is generally used to describe this function. Unfortunately the word *tutor* has also become widely used in secondary schools to describe the general pastoral guidance that teachers give to their students, as in *House tutor* or *Form tutor*. In this book we are using the term in its older connotation, of being concerned with the learning that takes place in the school. We shall refer to pastoral guidance as *counselling*, in order to avoid confusion. Of course, the two overlap.

The importance of tutoring is recognised and there is widespread commitment. Unfortunately this is not yet matched in practice. These are the problems:

- the problem of teacher time, referred to above

- the problem of inadequate resources to help mount substantial programmes of independent study

- the problem of training in the skills and techniques of tutoring.

The last of these is the one that teachers themselves can tackle. But it is a formidable task. Good teachers can become good tutors, but it is not as straightforward as many imagine.

The strong tradition of class teaching encourages teachers to build a repertoire of styles and techniques which are different from those required for tutoring. Making the shift requires deliberate action and a certain amount of persistence. Most require some personal assistance in order to succeed.

But this problem can be viewed as an *opportunity*. The cooperative nature of a development programme in tutoring is a stimulating experience and can bring benefits to a school staff far beyond the improvement of the techniques themselves.

This book has been written to achieve three things:

1) Define and describe what is meant by tutoring and make suggestions as to how tutoring might be gradually developed.

2) Analyse the components of tutoring and describe in detail what good tutoring might look like on the ground.

3) Suggest a programme by which a school staff might organise a staff development programme with quality tutoring as the objective.

1

Definitions and Justifications

DEFINITIONS AND JUSTIFICATIONS

A

A Stipulated Definition

The idea of tutoring is still fairly new, and a definition is always difficult for a concept which is still in its infancy. So this attempt should be regarded as provisional.

> Tutoring is the intensive support given to learners, usually in small groups, which is designed to enhance the quality of their learning. It recognises that learning is a subjective matter and so its role is to nurture, to encourage, and to minister to processes that are already going on within each student. Its repertoire of styles and techniques is a broad one, drawing on the best practice in teaching and counselling. Its long-term goal is the autonomy of the learner.

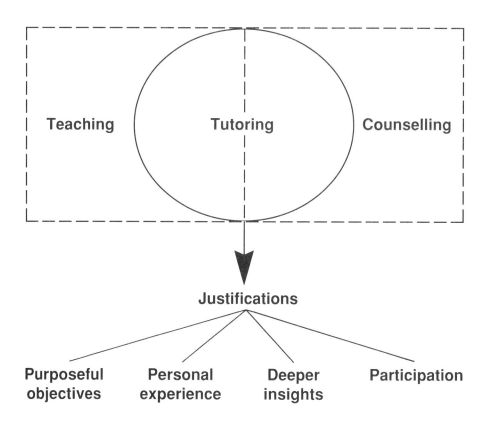

Definitions and Justifications

B ## Some Thoughts on the Definition

Tutoring v Teaching

At first sight it might seem that tutoring is nothing more than small group teaching. This is a mistake that is made by many on first attempts at tutoring. The differences need to be thoroughly understood.

- *Teaching* derives its style and techniques from the fact of large class size.

- *Teaching* has to be, for the most part, teacher-directed.

- *Teaching* can allow for only a limited amount of individual student participation, and this has to be largely teacher directed.

- *Tutoring* aims to cover a much wider range of styles and techniques than teaching. At the one extreme it can indeed be small group teaching, and no more. At the other extreme it can be almost entirely student-led, with the teacher playing only a minor role.

- *Tutoring* extends much more into the affective and social domains. In addition to being concerned with the students' intellectual development it aims to address itself to their personal and social needs.

- *Tutoring* is concerned with managing the students' individual work. This can be much more sharply focussed than the managerial tasks which are performed within class teaching.

- *Tutoring*, above all, emphasises the importance of the students' contributions. It is within the tutorial that they learn responsibility.

Tutoring v Counselling

Many have recognised that tutoring styles and techniques are similar to those employed by those engaged in counselling. Some important distinctions need, however, to be made.

- *Counselling* is usually, though not always, conducted on a one-to-one basis.

- *Counselling* focuses primarily on personal issues. Clearly these cannot be treated in isolation, but the focus is well defined and the counsellor will relate to other sources of information and help as required.

- *Tutoring* is usually, though not always, conducted with small groups.

- *Tutoring* focuses mostly on the students' learning , that is on their intellectual development. However, as we have already pointed out, there can also be a strong element of support for the students, personally, socially and in management terms.

- *Tutoring* therefore tends to be led by learning objectives. The good tutor will involve the students, as far as is possible, in the formulation of these objectives. But the role of the student is as a stake holder, not as the sole owner.

Tutoring v Independent Work

Many have seen tutoring simply as a supporting arrangement for students who are working independently. The main purpose is that the students should work independently and the tutorial has that as its only objective. This puts tutoring into an ancillary role and is an inadequate view.

- Independent work is a skill worth developing. But a lot of significant human endeavour is *inter*-dependent. It involves working as a member of a team, and collaborating with people, and working within systems of rules and conventions. So independent work should not be seen as the major purpose of education in schools.

- Tutoring does help students to work independently. But it has larger purposes. The tutorial is a training ground for team working and for taking on responsibility within our complex world of people, rules, and conventions.

C | Justifications

The tutorial is guided by well-defined objectives

This gives a structure and a sense of purpose. It helps give the tutorial an agenda, and so it takes on some of the attributes of a well-conducted business meeting.

The tutorial is a more personal experience for the participants

The main weakness of class teaching is that, with the best will in the world, it tends to be somewhat impersonal. The numbers make it so. On the other hand, the small numbers of the tutorial allow a much more personal approach. This means that each student can be more valued, and individual thoughts and feelings can count for more. The sense of belonging can be powerful. The result is that students feel that their learning is enjoyable and personally satisfying. They remember the contacts and the learning experience more vividly.

The tutorial enables the tutor to penetrate more deeply into the student's thinking and feeling

This means that the tutor can gain a better insight into the student's thought processes. Exactly how much is understood? Where are the confusions? Where is there lack of knowledge which is disabling? What does the student need to do? How will the student respond to suggestions? This all amounts to sophisticated diagnosis which is rarely possible in class teaching. But it also gives the tutor insight into the student's personal attitudes and feelings which can do so much to aid or hinder progress as a learner. The tutor can really claim to know the students in the group; and this is surely the first step towards helping them learn.

The tutorial encourages high levels of student participation

Because the numbers are small the tutor does not feel the need to lead the group all the time. The result can be that the action is shared evenly among the members of the group. Each individual speaks more, is invited to take on responsibilities, and stays alert. It is much more difficult to 'opt out'.

The tutorial is an educational experience in its own right

We have already argued that the purposes of the tutorial go considerably beyond supporting the students' independent work. Being a member of a tutorial group is all about being answerable, being active in learning, offering and receiving support, taking on responsibility, making commitments, reporting, arranging, questioning, debating, being questioned. This is where the students get their first real taste of what it means to be a responsible learner.

2

Early Training

Active Learning in Whole Class Teaching

The Use of Teams

Developing Independent Learning

The Way Ahead

EARLY TRAINING

The vision of a small group tutorial is an inspiring one. It is the ultimate ambition of many teachers. But there are problems! How can this be realised in today's conditions?

- class sizes are large
- students are not always sufficiently well-motivated
- there is a shortage of resources
- students lack the necessary skills of studying and organising
- students lack the confidence and skills required for effective oral communication
- teachers are not always clear about how they can shift from the traditional class teaching mode into a system involving the substantial use of small group tutorials.

These are real problems and there is no point in underestimating them. So it has to be accepted that the shift into the tutorial system needs to be made slowly and carefully. The whole process should be regarded as a progressive training for the students in participation and in the acceptance of greater responsibility. The teacher who says *My students couldn't cope with this sort of system* is probably right. But that is the challenge: how are teachers to move students from their present situation onto the road to greater autonomy?

The process needs to start as early as possible. In many primary schools the process has already started and secondary teachers would be well advised to find out how things operate in the final year of the primary school. Such an enquiry will often suggest how the process should be continued in the first years of the secondary school.

Basically the students need to get familiar with three things.

- ☐ Active learning processes.
- ☐ Team work.
- ☐ Independent learning.

These can all be introduced within class teaching. The basic idea is to shift the style gradually towards the small group tutorial.

Starting in the first year it should be possible to develop on these lines:

1) Increase gradually the number and sophistication of the active learning techniques used.

2) Emphasise increasingly the importance of team work.

3) Make greater use of independent learning assignments, by increasing their length, frequency and complexity.

By the time the fourth year is reached students should be competent in team work, able to plan and organise project work, and able to use effectively the support offered by the teacher and others within the school. This process is summarised in the diagram below.

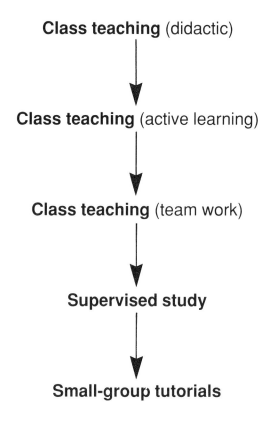

Class teaching (didactic)

Class teaching (active learning)

Class teaching (team work)

Supervised study

Small-group tutorials

Progress towards the Tutorial

A

Active Learning in Whole Class Teaching

This is described in more detail in the handbook in this series on *Classroom Management*. However, an outline of the main ideas here will help to give a picture of a smooth progression.

Justification

We justify the use of active learning techniques not only because they bring greater variety to the classroom. They are valuable in their own right, but have a greater significance because of the training that they offer.

- The students are given their first opportunities to make the decisions of the responsible learner, but always under the supervision and guidance of the teacher.

- The teacher is, through these techniques, developing a strategy which will overcome a tricky management problem - how to accomplish the shift from whole class teaching into an entirely different mode, namely the independent learning/tutorial mode.

Using Active Learning as part of a teaching programme

Wherever possible active learning techniques should be absorbed into the normal teaching and learning processes. They make their own distinctive contribution. A common sequence might look like this.

1) Normally a new topic might be introduced by whole class teaching. The teacher introduces the topic in a stimulating way, but also in a helpful way so that the students can begin to understand how the new learning will fit with their existing knowledge and how it will be structured.

2) Then the teacher might encourage the students to take a more active part through a class dialogue.

3) The next phase will introduce some active learning techniques, so that the students are thoroughly involved.

4) Finally the teacher will revert to whole class teaching in order to recapitulate and summarise.

There is nothing very revolutionary about that. But we are starting where the students are now.

Of course there can be many variations of this sequence and active learning could be introduced at any stage in the whole process. The important thing is not to miss them out! They can be far more effective

than the traditional form of class dialogue which can so easily
degenerate into a succession of short questions requiring one word
answers, with the teacher turning to one student after another in search
of the 'right' answer.

The Techniques of Active Learning

A fuller list is provided in chapter 4 of the handbook *Classroom
Management*, but a small selection is given here of those that are
particularly useful in the early stages.

Rough Paper

Instead of getting responses through
individuals in the traditional *hands up* manner,
it is useful to invite everyone to write down
their response. Then get them to share their
idea with a neighbour and examine the
similarities or differences. Those who have
discovered differences might then be asked to
describe them to the whole class. It is simple
enough, but a first step in learning to talk to
fellow students about the work.

Handouts

If handouts are issued they should leave
something for the student to do. If this is
explained at the beginning it helps to strengthen
attention to what is being said, and gives
a sense of ownership of the handout.

Student Questions

Shift the emphasis away from teacher questions
towards student questions. After a short
introductory talk there could be a pause in
which each student is asked to formulate a
question. It might be a question which
expresses a desire to have further detail, or it
might be an issue for discussion, or it might
be a question designed to clarify something
which has not been properly understood.
Students invariably need help in formulating
questions of this kind, and they should be
given advice and example. Always praise
good questions.

Silence

Teach them how to use short periods of silence.
They can quietly reflect and use the opportunity

to complete notes, look back over the work, prepare questions, etc.

The repertoire of active learning techniques can be gradually expanded from the modest list provided above. As students gain in confidence and in competence it will become apparent that they are ready to begin to work in teams.

B   The Use of Teams

When students have become accustomed to active learning they are ready for team work. Students need the opportunity to talk to each other about the work, to work collaboratively, to debate the issues, to have a sounding board for their ideas.

The Pair

The pair is a good first step towards team work, and it is an excellent arrangement in its own right. There are significant advantages.

- The pair can be formed on a friendship basis, which gives it a good chance for harmonious working.

- The pair is small enough for decisions about how to tackle the tasks to be made quickly and easily. The students don't spend much time discussing procedures or the allocation of tasks. They get on with the job. This is a great advantage with young and inexperienced students who often find difficulty in handling the complex relationships of the larger group.

- The pair fits in well with the use of teams for active learning. It operates as a sub-group within the team. So much activity can start in pairs and then graduate to the whole team. The teacher can vary the amount of time spent in the pair or the team according to the experience and capabilities of the learners.

- The pair retains a strong sense of personal responsibility for each individual student. It is so small as to give a sense of ownership. It offers encouragement and protection to the student who lacks confidence.

The Role of the Team

It is a nice arrangement where pairs are grouped to form teams. In large classes the best arrangement would be to group 3 pairs together to form teams of 6. Thus a class of 30 students would only have 5 teams. This is quite easy for the teacher to manage, and much better than trying to relate to 30 individuals, or even to 15 pairs.

Opinions differ as to the composition of teams. If friendship pairs are used as the basis for the teams this could produce teams which are fairly mixed and this might be the best solution. There seem to be dangers in extremes: on the one hand, a strong preference for ability grouping could create a difficult group of very low ability students; on the other hand, mixed ability arrangements might make the teaching of some subjects rather difficult.

In the handbook *Classroom Management* we argued the case for the *cabaret* layout of classroom seating. In this each team occupies its own table, with the members sitting round three sides broadly facing the teacher. The advantage of the 'cabaret' layout is that it can be a permanent layout lending itself equally to teacher exposition, class dialogue, paired activities, and team activities. The teacher can switch from one mode to another instantly. It provides an ideal training ground for the team activity which teaches the students some of the skills they will need in small group tutorials. It encourages the extension of techniques from the simple individual and paired activities into team work, but the extension can be accomplished carefully and cautiously. If tasks suddenly seem beyond the team's capabilities the teacher can quickly switch into an easier mode.

Since the team is the most important element in active learning and the basis on which subsequent tutorials will be built, it is vital to make sure that the teams work effectively. We are talking about *team building*.

We developed these ideas in the handbook *Classroom Management.*

- Give the team a short life-span
- Give every team member a job to do
- Emphasise that they are there to help each other
- Recognise the team's successes
- Reward them as a team
- Train them as a team
- Lead them towards self-management.

So we are trying to increase the level of motivation and gradually to increase the amount of responsibility that the team can take. It is a slow job and results will come mainly from practice and experience. You cannot 'teach' them about team work in theory and hope that they will be able to apply the principles in practice. We are talking about a range of complex skills which can only be built up slowly. But where a teacher believes in the ideas and has ultimate confidence in the students, the build-up will be noticeable.

As the team's skills increase so it will be possible to increase the sophistication of the active learning techniques used. We can now rely on the team's ability to organise itself and to engage in collaborative activity. At first the team tasks will be simple and short, but with increasing confidence they can become more complex and of longer duration.

Throughout, the teacher is in control of the situation - the teams report back to the teacher. So the teacher has total flexibility, switching from whole class work, to paired work, to team work, and back to whole class work, at will.

But within this safe context the students are making the most useful preparations for their later involvement in tutorial work.

C Developing Independent Learning

We have already argued that the tutorial is much more than a simple support mechanism for independent learning. Indeed the reverse argument needs to be stressed.

> The reason why we want our students to develop the skills of independent learning is so that the teacher can be freed to devote time to the intensive tutorial support of small groups of students.

Most teachers set their students small tasks to be done individually during ordinary class lessons. It relieves the teacher of having to be *on stage* the whole time, and offers the students a change of activity. There is nothing unusual about that. It offers the students a satisfying and beneficial experience.

But if we want to use the students' independent work as a means of establishing regular tutorials we have to be more ambitious. We need to increase substantially the amount and sophistication of such independent learning assignments. This will give us the discretionary time that we need.

In the handbook *Classroom Management* we examined in detail strategies which will help the teacher accomplish this ambitious aim.

- Make sure that any assignment material is clear and well within the reading capability of all the students. This is the material which gives the students *guidance* about what to do and how to do it. They must be able to cope with these with the minimum of support. So we should not regard these materials as comprehension exercises. Their function is strictly utilitarian. Assignments should be differentiated as much as possible so that each student is capable of achieving success.

- Try to have a *range of resource materials* which are sufficiently differentiated to meet the needs of all the students. Where a particular item is deemed to be difficult for its target group, supplementary guidance material can help make it accessible.

- Regard the *briefing* of the students as a most important occasion requiring the greatest of care. It is wise to get the students to demonstrate their understanding of the nature of the assignment before letting them start. In the early stages briefing will be directed at the whole class, and this demands extra care. It is so easy to allow individuals to detach themselves from the class thinking, only to require special help later on.

- Make firm rules about *access* to resources, equipment, and materials. The objective should be to eliminate all questions on these matters once the work has started.

- Make firm rules about *seeking help*. The teacher must not be the first person approached. Students must be taught to seek help first from other students. This can be operated on a free market basis, or restricted to pairs or teams if these have been formed.

The teacher's objective for independent work is to cut down the number of requests for help. This is not as perverse as it may at first sight seem. Much independent learning comes to grief because the teacher is inundated with requests for help and as a result becomes a *prisoner in the classroom*, unable to take any initiative because his/her time has been hijacked.

If the principles outlined above are followed the requests for help can be cut down. The teacher should only be concerned with really important and difficult questions. This is operating on the principle of *management by exception.*

How should the teacher's time be spent?

The first regular task is to **supervise**. This is usually accomplished by regularly going round the room checking that each student is on task and that no serious errors are being made. It serves also as a discipline to the students.

The second task is to **respond** to requests for help - those that have not already been filtered out by the strategies we have adopted. If the teacher is not too much under pressure, this is the opportunity to deal

The second task is to **respond** to requests for help - those that have not already been filtered out by the strategies we have adopted. If the teacher is not too much under pressure, this is the opportunity to deal thoroughly with a problem. There is much to be said for collecting together a small *ad hoc* group to listen and to help in the solving of the problem. This is the tutorial in embryo.

The third task is to **intervene**. This means helping an individual student or a small group to see the greater significance of what they are doing. It is about enriching their experience, or providing them with greater intellectual challenge.

D   The Way Ahead

The three strategies outlined above prepare a class for the tutorial mode:

- ☐   Active Learning
- ☐   The Use of Teams
- ☐   Independent Learning.

Everything hinges on the teacher's ability to gain more discretionary time. This is not easy and it does involve training students over a long period of time. But, if we are honest, we have to admit that we are sometimes our own worst enemies. We tend to have a great faith in our own ability to 'teach' them, and we judge a lesson by the amount of our own input. We are confusing teaching and learning; in our more reflective moments we have to concede that because we have taught something it is no guarantee that they have learned it!

This preparatory phase is so important that it would be worth while for a subject department to work out a long-term strategy to prepare students for tutorials. A document might contain the following information:

1) A summary of the present position for each of the year groups. What capabilities do the students already possess? What are the main weaknesses and needs?

2) A set of objectives for the current year for each year group. What capabilities do we wish to develop and how exactly will the training be accomplished?

3) A simple form of evaluation report at the end of the year.

In this way the drive towards the tutorial could be systematic and shared by all the teachers of a department.

The Basic Tutorial

Classroom Management

Style

Setting Objectives

THE BASIC TUTORIAL

In this chapter we look at the young student's first experiences of a tutorial. We assume that the early training described in the last chapter has been given, and that a class of students in the 11 to 14 age range is deemed to be ready to proceed further.

So our objectives for this chapter will have to be modest. We are working on the assumption that the class is a large one, that the students are inexperienced, and that the teacher wants to proceed cautiously, more interested in getting things on to a firm foundation than in making really bold leaps forward.

But in the pursuit of these modest objectives all the essential principles of tutoring will be encountered. So the chapter should be worth studying even by the teacher who feels that his/her situation allows a more ambitious approach.

The chapter is about the basic tutorial which is summarised in the diagram below. We shall save the more detailed analysis of the full potential of tutoring to later chapters of the book.

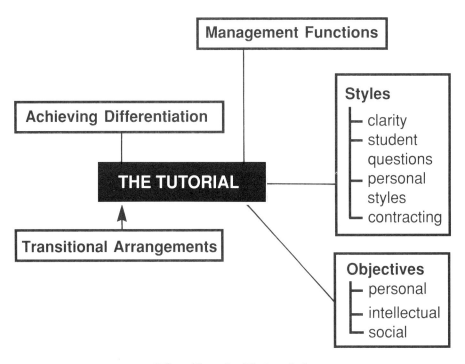

The Basic Tutorial

Classroom Management

The Starting Point

Let us start by defining our starting point in more detail. We are assuming that the students are familiar with active learning methods and for that purpose have been working in pairs which in turn have been combined into teams of 6 students. The seating in the classroom reflects this organisation, with the members of each team sitting together round a common table, able to work collaboratively or pay attention to the teacher as required. The teacher has devoted time to team building - encouraging the students to identify strongly with their team, and showing them how they can work together and support each other. In addition all the students are used to being set assignments to do individually or in pairs. Their work will be closely supervised and supported by the teacher, but there has been a deliberate policy of extending the size of the assignment to make greater demands on the their organising abilities. The teacher has made sure that the resources and assignments give the maximum support to the students, and has also built up a tradition of students seeking help from each other before approaching the teacher.

During the time devoted to supervised study the teacher has now found it possible to spend increasing amounts of time with individuals or small groups exploring issues more thoroughly. The small group is now the preferred way of working, and the teacher may, at different times, choose to use the existing teams which were set up for active learning, or to use *ad hoc* groups set up on the spot for a particular purpose.

The Main Problem

The main problem for tutoring in these large lower school classes remains. It is the combination of class size and the immaturity of the students. This creates two imperatives.

- The teacher's time must be used with great care. It is the most precious resource in the classroom and cannot be squandered. Time spent in administration or in resources organisation must be kept to a minimum. Time spent on the *substance* of the learning should be expanded.

- It must be assumed that for most of the time the students will be under the direct supervision of the teacher. Of course the teacher will always be on the look out for safe opportunities to release the students to other locations. Many schools, for example, have sound systems in place to enable individuals or small groups to visit and work in the library during class time. And there may be many other possibilities. It is important to know what the senior management considers to be safe and reasonable, bearing in mind the age and the sense of responsibility of the students in question.

The Transition from Class Teaching to the Tutorial Mode

How exactly do we make the shift from class teaching into the tutorial mode? There is scope for a real disaster here! Imagine the situation where a teacher is directing the work of the whole class and then decides to switch to the tutorial mode. He/she selects one of the teams for the first tutorial and starts a tutorial. But what are all the others doing? It would be unwise simply to rely on hastily contrived independent learning tasks, because we have already emphasised that success in working on such tasks depends on the quality of the briefing. We are on the horns of a dilemma!

So the technique must be to use the *supervised study mode* as a transition. Set the whole class an assignment and prepare them for it by very thorough briefing. Make sure that written assignments (if used) are crystal clear, and that the resources are accessible and very supportive. Test the understanding of the class before allowing them to proceed. Make the assignment a lengthy one, somewhere near the maximum that these students have proved capable of handling. Organise it for individuals, unless the students have already demonstrated their ability to work quietly in pairs. Choose a topic that is likely to be thoroughly absorbing.

When the class has settled and there is a good working atmosphere, the teacher should consider starting the first tutorial. The tutorial is to be a further briefing for a topic which follows naturally from the work that the students are now doing. It should be only a small assignment.

As a variation on this technique the teacher might prefer deliberately to deal only with one topic, dividing it into two parts: the first part being done through whole class briefing and the second part through briefing in each team's first tutorial.

In this first tutorial the teacher should work with one of the teams at its own table (any moving about the classroom should be avoided if at all possible). Explain how the new topic is related to what they are now doing. Explain that they are to move on to the new topic as soon as they have finished the existing task.

They must have paper on which to make notes, and it will be advisable to instruct them as to what they should record. They will need notes covering the decisions made and any instructions they may have been given.

Don't be afraid of being somewhat prescriptive in these early stages. The main priority now is **clarity**. They must come away from the tutorial with the feeling that they know exactly what to do and that they have useful notes to remind them of the essential details.

The tutorial must be very short, probably less than 5 minutes.

At the end of the tutorial give students the opportunity to summarise what they understand from the briefing and to ask any final questions.

They are now ready to continue with their present task, but also they are fully briefed for the next task and will be able to proceed naturally without any further intervention from the teacher.

Do not move straight into a tutorial with another team. Instead revert to the supervised study mode and do a tour of the classroom in order to check that students are on task and to respond to any problems.

Then the second team can be approached and the process repeated. Inside 45 minutes all the teams will have been briefed.

Maintaining the System

When all the teams have had their briefing tutorial the teacher can revert to the supervision and monitoring role, but remembering to insist that students must try to find solutions to their problems in the first place *within the team*. Increasingly now the teacher will find it an advantage to relate to the team as a whole rather than individuals, although there will obviously be many occasions when the help sought will be best given privately to the individual.

When a team appears to be getting close to finishing the task that was set in the tutorial, a second short tutorial should be given. At this stage in the students' experience it might be best for this tutorial to concentrate on *review* rather than another briefing.

The *review* tutorial gives the students the opportunity to report on the work they have done, the difficulties and the achievements. The tutor uses the differences which are apparent within the team and encourages the students to reflect on these. For some students it might be necessary to focus on serious weaknesses and to insist that a note be made to make sure that the kind of error is not repeated. But the most important need is for the teacher and students together to *react* to the work that each individual has done. *Recognition* is a most powerful motivator.

After each team has had its review tutorial a period of reflection and consolidation might be useful before embarking on further tutorials. So this has been a *short trial* - no more. During the period of reflection the students should be asked for their reactions to the experience, and they should be invited to make suggestions as to how the system might be improved.

The Problem of Differentiation

Many teachers will, during this first trial, have experienced a certain amount of untidiness in the system.

- The members of a team may have vastly different work speeds and this will result in staggered finishing times.

- Because they have all been set identical tasks the teams may all be ready for the review tutorial at approximately the same time, resulting in too many demands on the teacher's time.

- There may be a feeling that some members of teams are struggling with the task set and would have been better off with a different task. Likewise others may race through the work finding it insufficiently challenging.

- Compounding all the above problems there are likely to be a number of questions relating to the assessment of the work.

Now these are not new problems. They exist whatever system of teaching and learning is used. The tutorial system does however seem to bring them into sharp relief; we can no longer sweep them under the carpet!

In the long run the National Curriculum attainment targets, programmes of study and assessment arrangements will help teachers with these problems by providing a firm and clear structure within which to work. At the present time, however, it has had the effect of creating some anxiety by its exposure of the serious lack of differentiation in much classroom work.

So differentiation should be a major concern at this time, and the shift towards the tutorial system of teaching offers great possibilities. We are now recognising that a tutorial system must be flexible in operation. It should never be thought of as a simple mechanical system. It only works well when the teacher has enough imagination and flair to vary the details according to the dictates of common sense and the needs of the students.

Differentiation can be achieved in four ways.

1) By establishing a policy of selecting only those *resources* which for any given topic offer different data and stimuli for different levels of ability. Fortunately, under the influence of the National Curriculum the commercial publishers are beginning to respond to this need.

2) By creating a bank of *assignments* which is designed to act as a library of learning tasks which are differentiated for a range of abilities. (Book 3 *Resources for Flexible Learning* deals with this in great detail.)

3) By organising the *guidance* and *support* that learners receive so that tasks, resources, learning strategies, and expectations are matched to the needs and capabilities of individual learners.

4) By differentiated *assessment* so that student achievement can be recorded for different levels for any attainment target.

Differentiated resources and assignments are an important part of the armoury of the teacher who is developing student-centred learning. It is a big subject and is dealt with in the handbook *Resources for Flexible learning* which is part of this Teaching and Learning series. In this chapter we need to examine exactly how the teacher, acting as tutor, can offer differentiated guidance and support within the small team tutorials which we have already described.

Here are a number of suggestions.

Strike a balance between the whole group and the individual

Because we have determined to use the team of about 6 students for our tutorial work does not mean that they must always be treated as one unit. It is obviously economic of the teacher's time and effort when explanations, questions, and instructions can be directed at the whole group. But one of the really exciting possibilities for the tutorial is the way in which the students can learn to care about and support each other's work. So spend time during the tutorials with the focus on individuals. Involve the others in making suggestions or offers of help. So the group may be working towards the same attainment target but each individual may have slightly different tasks or use different resources.

Develop the tutorial as a flexible event, not a rigid one

We have implied so far that the tutorial is a continuous conversation between the tutor and the students. It need not be so. The tutor can often take out a little time to concentrate on the special needs of one student, while leaving the others with a small task to do or an issue to be discussed and resolved.

Have a desk plan of possible routes through the learning tasks

This amounts to a catalogue of the resources available and the assignments that have been produced, and could also include a few notes about library resources. This will mean that at any point in the briefing a student can be advised to use a different assignment, or alternative resources. A skilful classroom manager is not the *slave* of any course book, resource item or assignment however brilliantly it has been designed.

Make some private arrangements about additional support

Many teachers are anxious about the slow students and those lacking in confidence in any scheme which involves more independent work. They point out that such students often need more frequent attention than the occasional tutorial might offer. This is true and these students should be encouraged to check their progress more frequently with the teacher. They can do this quite easily during the times when the teacher is monitoring and supervising. The encounter need only be a brief one - the teacher checks that the student's progress so far has been on the right lines, and that he/she understands the next steps quite clearly. There is a marked improvement in the motivation and confidence of these students when this arrangement is adopted. Of course it is going directly opposite to one of the general principles we have laid down for independent work, namely that students should be encouraged to get help from other students before approaching the teacher. But this is the nature of classroom management. There are times when the principles must be sidestepped in the interests of the students.

Establish a contingency area

This might be an area in the classroom which is organised like a small resource centre, or it might simply be a box of additional resources and assignments. The purpose is to provide some rather special and interesting activities for students who, for one reason or another, find they need additional things to do. They may have completed an assignment and are waiting for a tutorial. Or they may have expressed strong interest in a particular topic and have negotiated with the teacher to allow them to enrich it. The materials need to be carefully chosen. Students should regard the use of the area as a prestigious activity.

Publish a list of maintenance activities

This could be displayed on a wall chart. Maintenance activities are the *housekeeping* activities of the classroom. Students should be taught to consult the list when they have small periods of unallocated time and to find a useful activity. Typical activities on the maintenance list might be updating personal logs or records, doing corrections, organising work folders, making contributions to wall displays, servicing resource areas, and so on. Between them the contingency area and the maintenance list should ensure that students do not sit wasting time.

B Style

Style is difficult to define. It is a mixture of many things:

* personal qualities
* habitual ways of dealing with and speaking to people
* habitual ways of doing things
* techniques in counselling and advising and teaching.

We should be optimistic about style. People can change their style if they are really determined to do so. But students can benefit from a wide range of styles, and should learn to do so. The drive may be ultimately towards the vision of the fully student-centred, enabling role, but many teachers are happier and very effective when operating in more modest styles.

The following suggestions are made for the teacher who is taking a class through their early experiences of tutoring.

In the early stages clarity is more important than choice

We have stressed the importance of getting the classroom management right, and, at the beginning, great clarity is the main need in the tutorial. The students need to learn the simplest tasks first, like delivering a piece of work in the place, at the time, and in the manner suggested. For many this represents quite a big step forward. There is little point in confusing them with decision making and choices before they are ready to handle them. So the pursuit of *clarity* becomes the main mission. Go for simple tasks and uncomplicated resources. Spell out the details of the information and the instructions. Get the students to describe their understanding of the assignment. In the early stages they must succeed, because nothing succeeds like success. When, and only when, they

have enjoyed this kind of success, are they ready to advance further
down the road to autonomy. Too many experiments in student-centred
learning have floundered because the teacher was too ambitious too
soon.

Start involving them through their own questions

Student questions are more important than teacher questions. All too
often a tutorial operates like a benevolent inquisition with the teacher
asking all the questions, trying to steer the students in the desired
direction. It is better to present them with a stimulus and invite their
questions. For example, the particular topic within the programme of
study might have some clear objectives. Let the students see these and
invite each one in a few moments of silence to formulate a question
which could be about meaning, about possibilities, about a perceived
problem. Then invite each student in turn to state his/her question and
invite the others to respond to it.

Don't answer their questions(!) - at least, not immediately

Note that it would be most unwise for the teacher to simply answer each
question with an instant solution. Nothing could so easily kill any
discussion at the outset. So, as a first step, get the team to try to provide
the answer. Then from the questions and from the team's attempts to
answer them the tutor is in a strong position to help the students make
their plans of work. As a result of the students doing the first thinking
about the work the chances of having it tailor-made to their needs are
much increased. The level of their motivation will also be much higher.

Maintain a warm and friendly relationship throughout

This is fairly easy when working with a small team. Always use their
names. At the beginning and end of the tutorial talk about things other
than the work, things in which you know they are interested. Be
tolerant of their mistakes. Defend them against any kind of aggression
or sarcasm. Set *ground rules* which forbid the destructive comment. Be
generous in your praise, but make sure that it is nicely measured - an
excess of fulsome praise will seem artificial and insincere.

Develop the tutorial in a business-like manner

So first of all get the students actively participating. Then the tutor
should give them firm and clear guidance about how they should tackle
the work. This means teaching them about the importance of objectives.
It means letting them see what is meant by high standards of work. It
means showing them how to take systematic notes so that they can

recall what has been decided and what they have committed themselves to do.

Conclude with a firm contract

Send them away from the tutorial with a feeling that they have formally contracted to complete a learning task in a particular way. They should be absolutely clear about it. Their notes will be the evidence.

There is a lot more to style than these brief notes indicate, but these are the important points for the early stages. We shall return to the topic for more detailed investigation in later chapters of the book.

C   Setting objectives

In the early days we have advised a cautious approach concentrating on clarity and firm guidance. But as the students get familiar with the method it is time to raise our sights. We shall now have an eye on the long-term goal of student autonomy. Our role as tutors is essentially a training one. We are out to show our students the techniques, styles, attitudes, and traditions of the mature learner. If the ground work has been done carefully the progress of the students will be rapid.

It is important in the early stages to share your thinking about student-centred learning with the students themselves. Take time to explain to them why you want them to work in this way. Point out the benefits to them. But it is generally better to emphasise to them the *hard sell* rather than the *soft sell*. This means that we focus on their practical needs: coping better when they are left on their own in higher education, making the best use of Open Learning opportunities in vocational training, being able to adjust to changes in employment, the unknown future. It means that we don't get sentimental about them having choice and making their own decisions. We certainly want them to do that, but is surprisingly easy to give a false impression of sloppiness and an abdication of responsibility, which the students can find quite alarming. So keep asking them for their evaluation of the tutorials. They can often make valuable contributions to the development of the tutorial style. They will get a sense of being involved in an important educational development and this will improve their motivation - the *Hawthorne Effect*, no less, but why not?

Good tutorials have clear objectives. Each tutorial may have unique sets of objectives, but there are kinds of objectives which recur many times. These are some of the objectives which might play an important part in the early development of the tutorial:

Objectives concerned with student participation

Gradually as the students become familiar with the method of the tutorial the teacher should aim to increase the level of their participation. Most of us seriously overestimate the amount of student participation in our class teaching; it is only when an impartial observer actually measures it that the reality comes to the surface. The same is true of tutoring. At the beginning it is worth offering some *don'ts* by way of advice.

- **Don't** start a tutorial with a *few words of explanation*. They will last longer than you intend and will put the students into a passive frame of mind.

- **Don't** believe that you can increase student participation by a few well designed questions of your own. For each question you will get a very short response and then they will all wait for your next question. This is the benevolent inquisition syndrome!

- **Don'**t answer any student questions. At least not immediately. Get the others involved before you make your own contribution.

- **Don't** be afraid of silence. It may mean that they are thinking!
Some of this advice may seem somewhat perverse, but we are trying to overcome the boredom and lack of motivation that is often so marked among adolescents. They need to be stimulated by being involved and by being given responsibility, **not smothered by the knowledge and assertiveness of their teacher**. Being aware of these pitfalls should enable the tutorial to develop on the right lines. When they become more active, then is the time for the teacher to match it with greater stimulus and challenge.

Objectives concerned with clarity of purpose

It is worth putting these objectives high on the list of priorities in the early stages. Some suggestions follow:

- For each task in the early stages - keep it short, keep it simple. This reduces the risk of confusion. We can develop the more complex assignments when students have learned how to cope with the simple ones.

- Check resources and assignments carefully for possible sources of confusion.

- Always encourage note taking during a tutorial. It may be necessary in the early stages to be prescriptive about what is written down.

- Always allocate time at the end for summarising and feedback. Make them say it back so that all possible confusions come to the surface now.

Objectives concerned with student cooperation

From a very early stage it should be possible to find opportunities for students to help each other.

- Encourage them to help each other within the tutorial itself. Get one of the students to help the one who is having difficulty, either privately away from the group, or publicly with the rest as friendly critics.

- Make arrangements for mutual support between tutorials. Act as a learning broker.

Objectives concerned with intellectual development

- Teach them the language of learning strategies - aims, objectives, hypotheses, tests, conclusions, conjectures, refutations, analysis, synthesis, evaluation, evidence, and so on. Encourage them to analyse their own thought processes. It is surprising how well quite young students can cope with this, providing we accept of course that their understanding of some of these concepts will be by no means fully developed.

- Persuade them to use measured and careful language in discussion of their learning tasks, in preference to colloquialism and slang. This needs handling with sensitivity, because we don't want to stifle their desire to contribute.

- Use praise frequently and focus on their attempts to structure their new knowledge in meaningful ways. If they are engaged in work which requires first hand observation show them how to handle anecdotal evidence in order to derive meaningful principles and generalisations.

People and Contexts

PEOPLE AND CONTEXTS FOR TUTORING

So far we have assumed that a tutorial is conducted by the subject
teacher within the normal class lessons.   There are however further
possibilities which we must now explore. We aim in this chapter to
answer two questions:

    ☐ Who tutors?

    ☐ In what contexts might tutoring take place?

We hope to show, as in the diagram below, that the world of tutoring is
much bigger than was implied in our previous chapter.

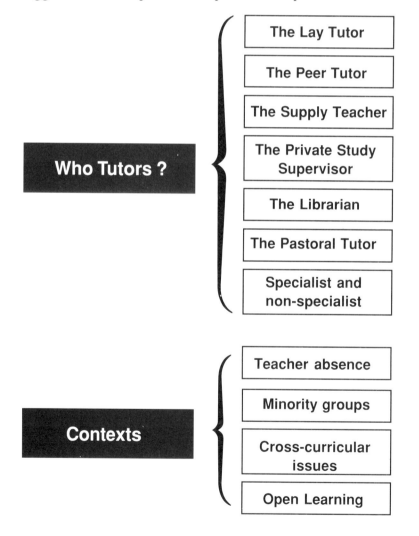

People and Contexts

A ## Who Tutors?

Specialists and non-specialists

Our secondary schools and colleges are organised, for the most part, around specialist teachers organised into subject departments. We naturally assume that tutoring will be fitted into the same arrangement.

Of course, the specialist teacher will be responsible for most of the tutoring in a school or college, because it will be a natural part of classroom work. The subject teacher is responsible for a whole programme of study and this includes all the planning and preparation and long-term guidance that the students receive. The subject teacher is a source of knowledge and experience for the students. In no sense could the subject teacher be replaced.

So the subject teacher will wish to develop the skills of tutoring and to train students from an early age, all within the context of the programme of study.

But we should recognise also that there is a tutoring role for the teacher acting as a non-specialist. At first it may seem that the non-specialist starts at a considerable disadvantage. He/she cannot hope to replace the specialist knowledge of the subject teacher. But there are some advantages which can prove to be valuable:

- The non-specialist does not threaten the student by virtue of vastly superior knowledge.

- The student feels more confident in discussion with the non-specialist because the student may know as much or more about the subject than the tutor.

- The non-specialist may not know the answers to students' questions. So the exploration in search of an answer will give the students time to think and make contributions. This is better than the instant answer that the specialist might be tempted to give.

- The non-specialist is much nearer the student in levels of understanding and will be able to become a co-worker in the learning process.

- The non-specialist constantly demonstrates to the students the styles, techniques and attitudes of the mature learner. He/she will teach them a great deal just by example.

If we recognise these advantages we must come to an important conclusion.

> Students will benefit from tutoring by non-specialists in addition to and as a complement to the tutorial support that they receive from their subject teachers.

This may imply that we need to change some of our ingrained habits. We are all, rather modestly, inclined to steer clear of discussion about subjects outside our own specialism. We act on the assumption that only the specialist must provide guidance and support. We seriously underestimate our own competence as educators in a *general sense,* over and above our specialism. We should shed our modesty and recognise that we are intelligent, highly articulate people, with substantial experience as learners and as teachers. We are familiar with the techniques of learning: - the analysis of meaning, the approach to problem solving, the skills of studying, and the benefits of perseverance.

But also life in schools and colleges can be very territorial! It may mean that we have to convince some of our colleagues that they really can benefit from the interest and support of others who are not specialists in their subject.

We shall be examining a number of possibilities for tutoring in which teachers will be acting as non-specialists. It will be helpful to make a few general points about this role before getting into detail.

Students must be told that the teacher is acting as a non-specialist

They must not get the impression that they are being fobbed off with something which is second-best. They need to see the positive reasons for the arrangement. So the teacher should explain the advantages of having *additional* support and that this will be *different* through being given by a non-specialist.

The teacher must have positive feelings about the arrangement

There should be no apologies. Instead there should be confidence that the students can be helped in a variety of ways.

The teacher should brush up on learning strategies and study skills

These are likely to be the most significant contributions that the teacher can make.

The teacher's questions can play a big part

This is an entirely different situation from the questioning done by a specialist (we have already discussed the dangers in this). The teacher's questions are not rhetorical or Socratic - the teacher may really need to know in order to understand. The students may be capable of providing the answers. This is the *co-worker* model. The teacher is setting an example of the mature learner at work. Students can often find this very stimulating and a boost to their confidence.

There are a number of contexts in which the teacher can contribute to the tutorial support of students by acting in the non-specialist role. We shall examine these in detail later in the chapter. But first we must extend the horizons even further.

The Lay Tutor

This is not such a new idea. In countless households throughout the country the parents of students of secondary age are recruited as *ad hoc* tutors when homework is being done. At its best this can be valuable. The parent does not aspire to be a subject specialist, but hopefully sits alongside the student and tries to help in understanding the unfathomable. The main contributions that the parent makes are asking useful questions, helping in the interpretation of difficult language, suggesting possible lines of approach, and generally being a sounding board for the student's ideas. Of course not every parent is so sophisticated, but many are. It can make a big difference to the motivation of a student and to subsequent performance.

Teachers are under such pressure that they should explore every possibility of using lay help whenever possible. We are talking mainly about parents, other students (peer tutoring), and members of the local community.

Of course there are dangers. Many lay people could do more harm than good. So the teaching staff will have to make an investment of some time in order to train the lay tutors, in the hope that the investment will eventually pay worthwhile dividends.

Generally it would be wise to judge the success of lay tutoring purely in terms of the gain in motivation and learning of the students. But teachers will recognise that there are also some valuable by-products in terms of public relations.

Peer tutoring is a special case. There are not only the benefits for the learners, but also for the tutors. We shall explore these in more detail later.

The general argument for lay tutoring is similar to that used for non-specialist tutoring, although the lay tutor will probably have less experience of such tasks.

We shall now look at specific applications of tutoring.

The Pastoral Tutor

The pastoral tutor has occupied an increasingly important position since the arrival of the comprehensive school in the fifties and sixties. Originally pastoral tutors were a response to anxieties about the increased size of schools and the possible loss of the personal touch. Good pastoral systems have embraced general welfare, educational and careers guidance, community activities, and records of achievement. More recently the pastoral system has played a leading role in developing personal and social education as a vital cross-curricular theme.

This is a heavy commitment, and the time allocated to pastoral tutors seems woefully inadequate. Also the groups are often quite large, and it is difficult to see how the teacher can accomplish much.

The problem has been compounded by the belief that many of the purposes of the pastoral curriculum have to be accomplished through one-to-one encounters. Clearly, one-to-one is necessary in some situations, but our general argument about the effectiveness of the small group tutorial should be carefully examined in this context.

This principle should be considered.

> Apart from those situations where personal privacy is the prime consideration, students' welfare, guidance, and records should be handled through small group tutorials.

We know the benefits of the small group experience: the sharing of information and ideas, the mutual support, the possibility of thoroughly individualising within the small group. There is also the practical benefit for the teacher in that the arrangement represents a more effective use of the teacher's own time.

There now exist many excellent schemes of personal and social education with rich resource material. (*Skills for Adolescence*, for example, is discussed in Book 3 of this series.) This opens up some exciting possibilities. Consider the following development in the pastoral system.

1) *Clarify the role of the pastoral tutor and the purposes of tutor time -* you will almost certainly have to be selective, unless the time allocation is generous.

2) *Adopt a scheme of work in PSE which is rich in student activities to be done individually or in pairs, or even in small groups.* Use this as the mainstay of the students' independent work done during tutor time. Use it to gain discretionary time for the tutor.

3) *Organise regular small group tutorials during tutor time.* Each tutorial will need to have clearly defined objectives which reflect the stage reached by the students. At certain times there may be specific needs such as major long-term decisions which have to made. At other times students could be asked to report on their progress in the PSE programme and make commitments regarding the next phase of this work. At other times the tutor may ask students to report on general progress in their academic work with emphasis on problems that are being encountered. There is a growing recognition that this is also the context in which *Records of Achievement* can be maintained. At first it may seem that these records should be done through one-to-one encounters. **The small group, however, offers better experiences for the students and is much more economic in the use of the teacher's time.**

So where the role of the pastoral tutor is deemed to be primarily concerned with educational guidance, it would seem highly desirable to extend this beyond the usual choices and decisions about whole courses. The pastoral tutor should be encouraged to get involved with the substance of the learning experiences now being encountered by the students. Students highlight their current learning problems. Some help might be possible within the tutorial time, or it may be possible to arrange for some private peer tutoring. Knowing that the pastoral tutor knows about and cares about the current learning tasks can be very reassuring. Much can be achieved.

The Librarian

Many schools do not have full time librarians, and it is difficult to see any scope in those situations where a teacher manages the library on a very meagre allocation of time. However for those schools that do have a full time librarian (or the full time equivalent) the possibilities should be fully explored.

Where the role of the librarian is properly appreciated the librarian is fully integrated into the educational programme of the school. He/she will play a part in curriculum planning and will be invited to contribute to departmental thinking whenever new plans are being made. There will be a good understanding of how the library will support the work of the departments. The librarian, in these circumstances,will make a direct contribution to the student's experiences through programmes designed to teach library and information skills. (The role of the library and the librarian is explored in more detail in Book 3 of this series.)

In many schools however the territory of the librarian is regarded as distinctly separate from that of the teachers. This is a pity because the librarian's skills in information seeking and handling should be made available to students on a regular and permanent basis, and it should be integrated with the mainstream subject work. It is not something that can be imparted in a single short course, once in a school lifetime.

We are talking, in effect, about the role of the librarian in the tutorial support of students. Many librarians stop short of really helping students in a sustained way because they feel they are straying into the territory of the subject teacher. They can justify their teaching of information skills, but tend to operate outside the main subjects of the curriculum, preferring the 'safety' of topics outside the school curriculum. They are wary of doing it clearly within the bounds of a particular academic subject. This is a pity, and librarians should be encouraged to explore possibilities in the same way as the teachers do as non-specialists.

There has been some valuable work done in the development of information skills in the secondary curriculum, and librarians have the understanding and the resources at their disposal to play a much more significant role than many do at present. They should be encouraged to extend their interests beyond the management of resources. They should be encouraged to acquire and practise the skills of small group tutoring. They should be recognised as active partners in the development of students' understanding *within* the subjects of the curriculum. Of course, the main problem is the familiar one of time. In a large school the job of managing the library and information services is a demanding one. However, there is a strong case to be made for recruiting ancillary help to take over some of the burden, leaving the librarian with more time to develop the support programme for the students.

The Private Study Supervisor

Private study used to be confined to the post - 16 student. With the arrival of GCSE and Standard Grade and with them the demands of course work and continuous assessment, some schools have wisely extended private study into the fourth and fifth years. It is always difficult to fit in the time with an overcrowded curriculum, but the advantages to the students are considerable.

Students need time to get on with their projects, but they also need time to consolidate, to work at problem areas, to catch up on work that may have been missed. These needs are over and above the homework which is set by the subject specialists.

So as a first step schools have put private study on the timetable. They have also recognised that it needs supervision.

But it would be a pity to let it rest there. The supervisor should be encouraged to play a much more active part than merely supervising the students. The organisation of a weekly private study period might develop on these lines:

1) In the first period the responsible teacher should explain a few things:

- the teacher is a *tutor*, not a supervisor

- the tutor will help in the *non-specialist* role

- each student needs to make a *work plan* for the next few (3?) periods

- the work plan should clearly be a response to *student needs* within the school curriculum

- each work plan should be *specific*, referring to particular needs and clear strategies for meeting them, and a list of the resource materials that will be used.

2) By the end of the first period each student will hand in the first proposals for a work plan. Students will be advised that they must come ready to start the work at the beginning of the second period.

3) Before the next period the tutor will study work plans in order to approve or suggest modifications. The tutor will also consider the possibilities of organising the students into self-help groups for the purposes of tutorials.

4) During the second period the tutor will invite the students to start
   work and will personally concentrate on any adjustments that are
   needed to work plans. After this is done it may be best to leave the
   students to get started, and simply to supervise and provide any *ad
   hoc* support that may be needed.

5) Subsequently the tutor may usefully conduct occasional tutorials or
   act as a broker in arranging some peer tutoring. It is not essential that
   the students in one tutorial group should all be doing exactly the same
   work. This is unlikely to occur. But they should nevertheless be
   encouraged to listen and make intelligent contributions to the work of
   others - it helps their understanding and consolidation of their work.

6) Later work plans will be made by each student as and when they are
   required. There is no point in trying to keep all the students in exact
   step with each other. So it will not be a clean mechanical system.
   There will always be a certain amount of untidiness, and much of the
   tutor's time will be spent setting up *ad hoc* teams for mutual support.
   Some students may find so much benefit from the arrangement that
   they may prefer to work independently all the time. In this context
   this seems reasonable.

In the end these students will know that their weekly private study
period will be a period of concentrated work with the possibility of
support through mutual aid. It should be a satisfying experience in its
own right, and it could do a lot for their examination results as well!

The Supply Teacher

Most schools have their own cadre of supply teachers. They provide a
vital support when teachers are absent through illness or through
professional activities which take them away from their classes.
Wherever possible supply teachers provide a specialist teaching service,
but they are also often asked to be much more versatile.

*It would be a good investment to have the supply staff trained in
tutoring skills.*

They may find themselves fortunately working with classes in their own
specialist subject where the regular teacher has been using the tutorial
approach. In such a situation the supply teacher would find it easier and
more productive to continue in this mode, without the necessity to
prepare additional material. The training that the students have had in
independent working will ensure that their teacher's absence for a short
time will have no adverse effects.

They may find themselves working with classes in subjects which are unfamiliar to them. In this kind of situation they should be encouraged not merely to supervise the class, because this can so quickly deteriorate into time-filling. Instead they should be encouraged to act in the role of non-specialist tutor. Set work to the class to be done independently (hopefully this will have been done by the absent teacher) and then invite groups to work with the tutor explaining what they are doing, discussing problems, and suggesting what is needed in the next phase.

In this way the supply teacher's work can become much more interesting, and the students will benefit more through this kind of activity than if they were simply working silently with supervision for the whole period of their teacher's absence.

The Peer Tutor

We shall examine two situations: the tutoring offered by students within the same class, and the tutoring offered by older students in a school for younger age groups (which is strictly not peer tutoring, but is usually given that name).

Within the same class

This arises quite naturally within the tutorials organised by the teacher.

- A student who has special knowledge or experience could be asked to conduct the whole tutorial for a short period.

- A student could be asked to give extra support to another student while the teacher is pressing on with the remainder.

- A student could be asked to give tutorial support to one or more students at a time and place which they would themselves arrange.

Students need to be prepared for these arrangements. The following suggestions could be implemented when suitable opportunities present themselves.

- The students should be in a constant dialogue about the ways in which tutorials are conducted. They must be encouraged to think critically. Their own experiences as students should help them to become better tutors.

- They should be made aware of the benefits of being a tutor - the challenge of thinking through the content and sequencing of subject matter, the challenge of diagnosing other people's problems and misunderstandings and the reinforcement of their own knowledge and understanding.

- They should be given a clear picture of the student-centred philosophy, and guidance about the techniques that encourage greater student participation.

When peer tutoring is well established within a class it should become a normal part of the review process, so that the sense of responsibility of the peer tutors is enhanced and the importance of the activity recognised.

When peer tutoring is well established it helps create a sense of a *learning community* which is surely what education is all about. This is very ambitious, of course. But this is the general direction in which we should be heading.

Tutoring by Older Students

The same general principles apply to this kind of situation. But there are some additional points about the contexts. The experience of tutoring can be an integral part of the tutor's own education.

- Students who have made career choices within the helping and caring professions.

- Students who need opportunities to develop themselves in terms of becoming more responsible, or more articulate, or more outgoing. Having a real job to do can often work wonders.

- Students who, as part of their own studies, need to have access to a 'target population'. The design of these arrangements needs to be carefully done, but they can be very influential.

There is one kind of tutoring which has been carefully developed in many schools, and that is the tutorial support of young slow readers (11-12 years) by older low achievers (15-16 years). This is often organised on a one-to-one basis, and benefits are claimed both for the student and for the tutor.

In some instances the tutors are given intensive training and supervision by the special needs staff to help them support the young students in an unstructured way. In other instances the tutors are given a very short training in a form of *programmed tutoring* in which they are required to follow a prescribed programme step by step. It is interesting that in the latter great emphasis is placed on the *pause* - waiting a given length of time or for a signal from the student before taking the next step which is the *prompt.*

The main message from the programmed tutoring systems is that some of the skills of tutoring can be passed on to peer tutors by setting limited

objectives and analysing exactly the kind of skills the tutor is expected
to use. Teachers who are experimenting with all kinds of peer tutoring
would do well to see some of the programmed tutoring systems in
operation. The scope for extension of some of the principles seems
good.

The great benefit of using all kinds of peer tutoring is that it is a form of
delegation. Delegation seems to be vital for teachers who want to
develop more individualised systems of learning and who want to shift
their own styles towards tutoring. They need all the help they can get.

Parents

We made the point at the beginning of this chapter that many parents
already act as tutors to their offspring, that is, in the academic sense as
well as the personal sense. We have also sought to justify the tutor who
is a non-specialist and the tutor who is a lay person. The parent
combines both these, advantages and disadvantages alike.

It would be worthwhile for a school to try to make the best possible use
of this reservoir of commitment and energy. Parents are so often only at
the receiving end. Many would welcome some positive guidance on
how they might contribute. This might take the form of printed
guidelines, or even some systematic training.

The main thrust of any such guidance will naturally be towards the
enabling role that we have already described for the non-specialist. It is
also interesting that a number of schools now involve parents as tutors
of their own slow-reading offspring, using programmed tutoring
schemes.

It will be no bad thing for many parents to think through these roles.
Too many are still believers in the *mug and jug* system of education (all
you have to do is to fill them up with knowledge!). But if they are
properly advised and helped they will recognise that the skills of good
parenting are the ones that are needed in education as well.

Members of the Local Community

Schools often tap this reservoir of knowledge, skills, and experiences.
They invite local people to come into school to talk to groups or to
become involved in the students' activities.

Using some of them as occasional tutors could be valuable. Sometimes
such people are called *mentors*, to recognise the fact that they are there

to provide specialist knowledge which is in addition to the main tutorial support which is being given by the teacher.

The same principles apply as for the parents. It may be that the danger of the over-didactic person is greater in this group. The person invited may be an enthusiast or an expert, and believes that he/she is being invited to communicate that expertise in as short a time as possible. The temptation to try to 'tell them' quickly is difficult to resist. And this could be followed by disillusionment if the students do not instantly share the enthusiasm. So careful selection and careful induction may be the order of the day.

One particularly useful technique with this kind of lay tutor is to focus on the student questions. Set the tutorial up as a one-person brains trust, with the students asking the questions that concern them. But where the tutor is sympathetic to the school's broad aims for tutoring, the range of styles can be much wider.

B Tutoring Situations

Of course the classroom and the timetabled classes are the most important situation for tutoring. But people other than the subject teacher can contribute to the support of the learner, and much learning can and should take place outside the classroom. All this suggests that we should look briefly at other tutoring situations.

Teacher absence

Teacher absence caused by illness or by professional activities can present problems. The choice has always seemed to be between supervision (assuming that work has been set by the absent teacher or by a colleague in the department) or a maintenance of the teaching programme by a supply teacher. Prospects of keeping a sense of continuity are better if the class is accustomed to working in the independent learning/tutoring mode. Tutorial support can be continued by a teacher acting in the role of non-specialist, or by a supply teacher who will not have to hastily prepare material but will be able to pick up the reins in a more relaxed way.

Minority group needs

Even when the National Curriculum is fully implemented there will still be options 14-16, ans some may be offered which go beyond the 10 foundation subjects. Occasionally an option on offer may attract only a minority of students, yet the school may retain a conviction about its desirability.

This is the situation which prompted the setting up of the supported self-study project in the early eighties. It is reasonable to argue that if the numbers in a group are very small the subject should be tackled in reduced contact time relying on independent learning supported by intensive tutoring. It should be noted that the relationship between class size and amount of contact time is not a simple one. The teacher needs a fixed amount of time for planning, preparation and general administration of the course regardless of class size. But there are also variables (marking, monitoring, and assessment) which are much smaller when the class size is decreased.

Cross-curricular issues

Similar arguments apply to cross-curricular issues. The time demands of the National Curriculum combined with the universal desire to preserve cross-curricular elements are combining to put considerable pressure on school and classroom management. It is likely that schools will prefer to *embed* rather than *bolt on*! This means inviting each subject department to make its own distinctive contribution to the cross-curricular dimensions, skills and themes.

All this will make bigger demands on the students' responsibility and capability in independent learning. They will need the support of high quality tutoring skills.

The teacher is likely to, and indeed has to, become much more productive. It is interesting to note that many of the early anxieties of teachers that systems like supported self-study would lead to a more *laid back* approach, have given way to a recognition that, in skilled hands, the very opposite could be true.

The developments proposed for the 16 to 19 age groups are now presenting the same kinds of problems and opportunities. There is the widely publicised desire to make firmer links between academic and vocational education, allowing for the development of a range of *core skills*. Here it is likely that schools will continue to offer some *bolt on* arrangements, such as General Studies, while exploring the possibilities for achieving more within the main courses of study.

With the increased maturity of the students the possibilities for the independent learning/tutoring system seem very great indeed. There is a strong case for using a General Studies programme as an exemplar in the school or college for the supported self-study style. The topics lend themselves well to the investigative approach organised on individual or small group lines, especially with the support of study guides like those produced by Network Educational Press. (See Book 3 *Resources for Flexible Learning* for a detailed analysis of study guide use.) The tutorial should be a powerful integrating force, and the remaining chapters of this book should offer some pointers as to how the tutorial could be developed.

Open Learning

There have been few developments of Open Learning within the secondary sector. Open Learning is characterised by the open access it offers to students free from institutional constraints. Students make their own decisions about the time, place and manner of the work. Heavy reliance is placed on the open learning 'package' of learning resources, and tutorial support tends to be not as frequent as in most school contexts.

There is a case for making use of these kinds of arrangements, particularly where a student, for one reason or another, requires a programme which is strictly individual. It is a good experience for an older student, anticipating the open learning experiences which are bound to follow in adult life.

5

The Objectives
of the Tutorial

Intellectual Objectives

Attitudinal Objectives

THE OBJECTIVES OF THE TUTORIAL

We have already made the point that the tutorial is much more than a simple support mechanism for independent learning. It is an educational experience in its own right. We have gone further and claimed that high quality tutoring offers greater potential for improvements in school education than any other single strategy.

These are bold claims. So we must now try to justify them by analysing the educational objectives that guide our work in tutoring. But the objectives which we shall describe are not likely to be unique to tutoring. They are those that are written into the National Curriculum, and in the statements which support recent initiatives in education such as TVEI, CPVE, Standard Grade and the GCSE.   These objectives are summarised in the diagram below.

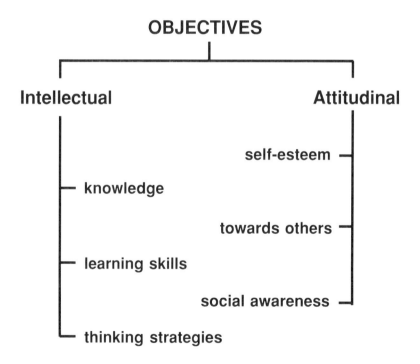

Tutorial Objectives

So our concern must be to demonstrate how the tutorial can be a particularly effective way of achieving them. What new capabilities and what new attitudes does our programme of study hope to produce? In the simplest terms, what differences do we hope to see as a result of our efforts?

A Intellectual Objectives

Knowledge

The student acquires a great deal of information in the course of a school career. This is very important, and we should not allow our current preoccupation with skills to lead us to neglect the student's need for knowledge. Knowledge is knowing *about*, a skill is knowing *how*. They are not mutually exclusive, they are interdependent.

In this section we are talking, quite simply, about facts, names, and events, together with the generalisations which are made about them. We are talking about *who*, and *what*, and *where*, and *when*, and *how*.

Many students are anxious about their knowledge. They are all too aware of their ignorance compared with their teacher. They feel a lack of confidence when they are asked to engage in discussion without a firm foundation of knowledge on which to base it. The knowledge we are discussing now is simply verbal information. It is acquired through reading or listening, and its existence is proved by speaking or writing.

It would be wrong to despise the acquisition of knowledge. Some educationists have made the error of implying that the 'mere' acquisition of knowledge has little to commend it. They have given the impression that all learning which is concerned with simple knowledge must be rote learning. We cannot let our students down by adopting this sterile philosophy. We must use the tutorial as an occasion for a very different approach to knowledge acquisition.

So within our tutorials these are some of the indicators that might tell us that our students are building a sound base of useful knowledge:

The students display a high degree of motivation

They want to increase their knowledge and understanding, and cooperate readily towards this end.

The students are stimulated by the information, ideas and materials

Such stimulants can help students to overcome their initial difficulties when handling concepts and ideas which are new.

The students are capable of being selective

They learn to pick out what is crucial to the rest of the knowledge. They learn to identify what is of particular importance to them in their own programme of study.

The students are capable of structuring their new knowledge

They do not treat the facts and ideas in isolation from each other, but rather see that they are related to each other or dependent on each other. They know how to use diagrammatic techniques to summarise the structure of their new knowledge.

The students can demonstrate how the new knowledge fits in with knowledge and understanding which they have acquired previously

This is skilled building work! If the students can appreciate these relationships there is a better chance of them retaining the knowledge.

The students perform well in the recall of the knowledge

They have developed their own techniques: mnemonics to help in the simple recall of facts, and the use of structures to support the recall of larger bodies of information. They are sophisticated in their approach to testing, and accept testing as a regular feature of their school work.

The students can demonstrate how to transfer their knowledge

They can apply their new knowledge in new situations or contexts. They know how to frame questions which will help them do this.

The students are capable of demonstrating their knowledge

They can make extended presentations to fellow students or to other audiences. Demonstrations of this kind can be a powerful reinforcement of learning.

The students know how to handle feedback from the tutor

The tutor is constantly conveying to the students information and judgement about the standards they are reaching in their knowledge and understanding. This should give the students a clear vision of what stage they have reached and what the additional needs are.

The students develop their skills as self-managing learners

Of course, much of the early activities of a tutorial will rely heavily on the tutor's lead. Gradually the students must be encouraged to take on these responsibilities for themselves. They must learn to supply their own motivation, develop their own structures and procedures for handling knowledge, and be keen to demand opportunities to demonstrate their knowledge and to get feedback about it. At a later stage on the students' journey towards autonomy the teacher will intervene much less, but the interventions will be about major issues and about changes of emphasis.

The aim of our student-centred approach to education is progressively to increase the responsibility which we give to our students. The art is to judge what is right for any given group of students at any given time.

Learning Skills

A skill is simply the ability to do something which is useful or satisfying. It is concerned with action, with knowing *how* as opposed to knowing *about*. But, of course, knowledge and skills are often mutually dependent. Many skills can only be applied through knowledge.

Skills are ingrained in our lives. We practise a wide variety constantly. They spread across all aspects of our lives - intellectual, emotional, social, and physical. It is not surprising that we talk about 'Life Skills'.

Adopting skills as educational objectives, however, needs to be approached with caution. The danger is that we will slip into the error of teaching them, in the belief that all students need is to *know* about them. A more elaborate definition will guard against this danger.

If we reflect on some common skills, whether intellectual, personal, social, or physical, we shall be struck by the fact that they can be performed to a high level *without the performer necessarily being able to state the rules that govern that high performance*! Take the riding of a bicycle as a simple example. Is it necessary for a learner to be able to explain the forces at work when he/she is trying to balance the bicycle? The child will not attempt to do such a thing. Instead, balance will be achieved by the feel of it. So our achievement in skills is a mixture of knowledge, experience, intuition, and feel, but above all practice.

There is a message in this for all who are interested in helping young people to acquire new skills. **Experiences** should be at the heart of this learning process. They need opportunities to learn on the job, and this means some trial and error, lots of practice, and opportunity to reflect on their progress. This is not to deny the importance of two support activities. One is the teaching of specific *techniques*. The other is the personal *counselling* which can make such a big difference to students who are attempting to get to grips with new skills.

We shall look at two categories of learning skills: study skills, and information skills. There is considerable overlap between these two, and also between them and the thinking strategies which form the subject of the next section.

Study Skills

Every teacher must be a teacher of study skills, and this is even more true when students are working independently supported by regular tutorials. It is not a question of setting time aside occasionally to talk about study skills. It is more a matter of introducing techniques and advice whenever the students seem ready for it and in need of it.

Without going into details of the techniques involved, here is a check list of the skills which should be developed in the students:

a) **Reading Skills**

- The ability to make use of the support devices offered by the author and publisher - the 'blurb' on the cover, the preface, the chapter headings, any summaries or the index.

- The ability to practise the art of skimming - getting the general gist of a chapter by picking out the significant words and phrases.

- The ability to practise the art of scanning - finding specific information by using the index, or by conducting a visual search through material.

- The ability to make notes as they read.

b) **Listening Skills**

- The habit whenever they are listening to anyone of having a pencil at the ready, and writing down, at the minimum, some of the key words.

- The ability to discover the structure of the speaker's talk if it has not been made explicit.

c) **Note Taking Skills**

- The recognition of the value of note taking as an essential survival technique in all sorts of situations.

- The ability to write notes that summarise, pick out key words and phrases, and generally support the learner during revision.

- The appreciation of the possible visual impact of good notes - use of space, helpful layout, extra marks for emphasis (underlining, boxes, circles, capitals, stars, arrows, etc).

- The understanding of the techniques of patterned notes.

- Knowledge of systematic ways of storing and retrieving notes - use of files and simple classification schemes.

d) Writing Skills

- An understanding that careful thought must always be given to the purposes of a piece of writing. Who is to be the reader? What are you aiming to achieve?

- An appreciation of the importance of planning: brainstorming followed by sorting ideas into a coherent structure, for example.

- An appreciation that writing needs to be read critically before being submitted.

e) Organising Skills

- The ability to use simple time management techniques - use of 'things to do lists', personal incentives, etc.

- The ability and determination to make long-term plans - relating to course work, examination revision, etc.

- An advanced state of personal awareness - strengths and weaknesses.

f) Questioning Skills

- An appreciation that asking questions is the mark of a good learner, not a sign of ignorance.

- An appreciation that questions are not only about facts. Some of the most useful questions are the result of pondering or wondering or speculating.

g) Presenting Skills

- The ability to present the results of work in interesting and helpful ways.

Information Skills

There is considerable overlap between study skills and information skills. Generally, however, when thinking about information skills we concentrate on the student's need to find out, particularly in situations where there is a large range of possible sources. So information skills are often at work in the school library or in a departmental resource centre, or when information technology is providing the sources of information. But the principles are applicable wherever teaching and learning are taking place.

But we need to look wider still to fully understand the significance of information skills. Information is the means by which people broaden their horizons and enrich their lives. It enables them to make better choices and decisions in whatever circumstances they find themselves. So it would be wrong to think of information skills as an exercise exclusive to the school library. Information skills are life skills - they are a necessary entitlement for all our young people.

a) **Library and IT Skills**
The student is able to use the keys and tools of the library and IT systems. The student must have both knowledge and some subordinate skills.   Each student should:

- Know the layout of library and IT areas

- Know the rules for the use of these areas

- Know what resources are available and understands the storage arrangements

- Be capable of using the subject index and catalogues

- Be competent to handle the IT equipment

- Be able to load and use IT software

- Be able to use reference works to get an outline understanding of a topic and to organise a programme of study.

b) **Assignment Skills**
Nine steps were proposed in a curriculum bulletin of the former Schools Council, and these have been influential in a number of schools. Expressed as skills the steps are as follows:

- Can formulate and analyse need

- Can identify and appraise likely sources

- Can trace and locate individual resources

- Can examine, select and reject individual resources

- Can interrogate resources

- Can record and store information

- Can interpret, analyse, synthesise, evaluate

- Can present and communicate

- Can evaluate.

Thinking Strategies
One of the most significant characteristics of a mature learner is that person's awareness of his/her own thought processes. This is the basison

which rational judgements are made, leading to responsible decisions. Young people need help in acquiring these insights and capabilities. How we learn and how we think should be regular features of tutorials.

We have already dipped into this topic in the previous section through our consideration of learning skills. But more needs to be said about the ways in which the tutor and students can interact in order to help the students on their journey towards intellectual maturity.

We are grouping the strategies under four headings: elaborating; monitoring; organising; and inventing.

Elaborating Strategies

These occur when students seek ways of extending, deepening, or simply clarifying the concepts and ideas which they are using. A number of capabilities contribute:

a) **Paraphrasing**

The student can demonstrate growing understanding by expressing an idea in different words.

b) **Summarising**

The student can select the important points and use them to make a comprehensive summary.

c) **Seeing the consequences**

The student may express this as likely results, or opportunities, or threats, or choices, or possibilities, or constraints.

d) **Finding a place for the new learning**

The student relates the new knowledge to previous well-structured knowledge and identifies its significant contribution.

Organising Strategies

These occur when students make a conscious effort to provide structures for their knowledge or to determine procedures for handling it.

a) **Grouping**

The student consciously arranges facts, concepts and ideas into meaningful groupings. This is the activity of classification and categorisation.

b) Ordering

The student seeks to establish a sense of order in the new knowledge. This may mean establishing priorities, or ranking, or devising sequences.

c) Establishing relationships

The student will seek to identify cause and effect, or dependency, or inter-dependency.

d) Applying logical reasoning

The student will make use of deductive reasoning (deriving a conclusion from what is already stated in the premises), and inductive reasoning (using evidence to arrive at a conclusion with varying degrees of certainty).

e) Developing strategies for problem solving

The student is capable of tackling a problem in an intentional way, as opposed to using unorganised trial and error methods. This will involve familiarity with the concepts of conjecture, analysis, and synthesis.

f) Using 'balance sheets' to help organise thinking

The student can carefully develop two opposing views about a topic by putting them alongside each other. This may be done by writing in two adjacent columns. Examples of column headings are: strengths v weaknesses; advantages v disadvantages; gains v losses; benefits v costs; opportunities v problems.

Inventing Strategies

These occur when students recognise that invention plays a part in learning, and that where answers are not known, it is useful to practise bold conjecture.

a) Using divergent thinking

The student is capable of asking questions which go beyond the facts. These are the 'What if...?' type of questions.

b) Using intuitive thinking

The student is not afraid to think intuitively and has a good understanding of the role of intuitive thinking in an overall thinking strategy. A most frequent use of intuitive thinking is at the start of problem solving, especially if the problem seems to be an intractable one. Intuitive thinking gets the process started and helps the student to appreciate the provisional nature of the activity.

Monitoring Strategies

These occur when students demonstrate their ability to monitor and control their own learning activities.

a) **Using self-questioning**

The student is capable of monitoring his/her own work. This involves the determined use of self-assessments of all kinds and frequent reflection about progress and styles.

b) **Managing the learning process by objectives**

The student understands the value of careful objectives in studying, and is capable of developing such objectives and using them as a guide and a discipline.

B Attitudinal Objectives

Self-esteem

The student's own self-image is a major factor in the student's educational achievement. Of course there is always a gap between the ideal self (the person the student would like to be), and the real self. This is in itself is often quite marked in adolescence. But the tutorial can be a powerful force for good helping each student to develop in the following ways.

The student knows his/her own academic capabilities

It is a question of balance. The student is not too self-critical, leading to a lack of confidence and too much anxiety. Nor is the student thoughtless and over-confident so that the lessons that life has to offer (both the academic and the social) are spurned.

The student is in control of his/her own emotions.

This means being able to handle the more traumatic of school experiences, particularly the great success and the great failure.

The student is aware of his/her personal strengths and weaknesses.

As a result the student is frequently observed building on the strengths and using them to overcome the weaknesses.

The student is accustomed to set realistic personal goals

This results in a calm and measured approach to work and inter-personal relationships.

Consideration towards others

The student finds that cooperation and the giving and receiving of support come naturally.

The student takes pleasure in working as a member of the group

This emerges as pride in the group's achievements, and an eagerness to accept different roles within the group's organisation.

The student readily offers support to other students

This is at its best when it is not only offered but sustained over a period of time, including out-of-school time.

The student accepts help from other students

Help is accepted with gratitude and with a constructive attitude.

Awareness of and response to social realities

The student relates to the social realities at all levels from the group to worldwide issues.

Within the group the student displays sensitivity to the personal needs of individuals and to the principles of equal opportunity

A wide range of behaviours results from this response - listening, supporting, accepting, encouraging.

The student displays an awareness of and response to the great social concerns of our times

This manifests itself in sincere seeking of information, thoughtful responses, and positive thinking about possibilities.

6

Managing the Tutorial

Objectives and Agendas

Student Responsibilites

MANAGING THE TUTORIAL

We have emphasised how the role of the teacher changes when the tutorial role is adopted. The new role consists of the following:

- helping the group and individual students to set clear objectives for each learning task

- helping the group to work effectively as a team during the tutorial

- supporting the group with information and ideas about resources

- helping the group and individuals to make useful work plans

- encouraging active participation of group members and mutual support

- setting an example of a disciplined intellectual approach to the work.

This means that the teacher is now combining three basic styles:

- ☐ the style of the manager
- ☐ the style of the personal counsellor
- ☐ the style of the academic mentor.

In this chapter we analyse the tutorial from the point of view of the *manager*. It is summarised in the diagram opposite.

A   ## Objectives and Agendas

Every tutorial should have clear objectives. We are talking here about the objectives for the tutorial, and these should not be confused with the longer-term educational objectives which we have for our students (those that were described in the last chapter). Of course, the two are closely related.

The objectives of the tutorial are simply designed to answer the questions:

What is the purpose of this tutorial?

What do we want this tutorial to achieve?

Like all good objectives they should describe the desired *results*, or *achievements*, or *differences* rather than simply describing what is going to happen.

When the objectives are clear then we can describe what is going to happen. We produce an agenda.

Agendas

- Briefing
- Review
- Discussion
- Coaching
- Short-term planning
- Long-term planning

Student Responsibilties

- Research
- Records
- Correspondence
- Organisation
- Process observer
- 'Expert'
- Evaluation
- Agenda setting

Management

The agenda of a tutorial is not likely to be an elaborate affair. There may be only one or two main items on it. Here are some of the items which might appear on the agenda of a tutorial.

Briefing

This is the discussion and instructions which *precede* any new work. It is vitally important in the support of independent learning. Students usually need this advance support and it can make a significant difference to their attitudes and their performance. Neglect of it can lead to confusion and poor performance.

The briefing should include a consideration of:

- the learning objectives

- the nature of the task set

- the resources to be used

- the general approach to the work

- the problems and special opportunities that are likely to be encountered

- the nature of the outcome - eg. the presentation of written work with indications about its length and style

- the contract between tutor and students, which details all the agreements about times, places, outcomes, etc.

Briefing can sound like a very prescriptive activity, and it can be so when the students are inexperienced. But the tutor is constantly seeking opportunities to raise the level of the students' participation and mutual support. This aspect of briefing will be discussed in the next chapter.

Review

This is the discussion which *follows* the completion of a piece of work. It is often valuable if, during the prior briefing, the students can be instructed to hand in their work before the next tutorial to give the tutor the opportunity to review it and assess it.

Another valuable advance arrangement is to get a pair of students to exchange work with a view to them being able to contribute to the review of each other's work.

There can be many variations on these themes. The intention is clear - to make arrangements which will increase the level of student participation during the review tutorial.

The review itself can include the following:

- An individual student reports on how the work was done, what was learned, what problems were met

- A student is invited to report on the work of another student

- The tutor organises discussion about the problems raised

- The tutor invites a student to make suggestions about the assessment and then gives his/her own report.

A review tutorial is likely to be somewhat more difficult to handle than a briefing tutorial, because the work being reviewed has often been done individually. The tutor must guard against being drawn into detailed discussion with one student to the exclusion of the rest. This means using the observations, reflections and suggestions of the other students as much as possible. This is immensely valuable to them - an opportunity to consider quality and performance in a detached way without being the centre of attention. Students can learn a great deal by worrying about other people's problems.

Discussion

Discussion takes place within all agenda items in a tutorial. But discussion can be an agenda item in its own right. Time is simply set aside for a more thorough exploration of issues and problems.

In this kind of tutorial the students will particularly welcome advance notice of the agenda. They can prepare themselves by finding out relevant information, or by thinking of issues, problems and arguments.

If the topic is a big one it is better to break it up into a sequence of headings or questions. These should be notified in advance so that the group as a whole will regulate itself by sticking to the agreed agenda.

Coaching

Coaching, which is simply intensive *teaching*, can be a valuable use of tutorial time. It focuses on difficult problems or on special issues. It differs from class teaching because of the advantages of the small group.

So the tutor's explanations will be more accurately tailored to the needs of the group and to individuals within the group. The tutor's questions will be more penetrating and more persistent, aiming to diagnose with great accuracy any signs of misunderstanding. The students will be expected to sustain their own contributions much more, and to assist in the processes of analysis and diagnosis.

In some instances great power can be invested in a coaching session by declaring at the outset a standard of mastery to be achieved by every member of the group. This helps to create a sense of shared purpose and determination, which is much healthier than the sense of inquisition which intensive coaching sessions can induce.

Short Term Planning

With the increasing emphasis on project work in the curriculum many of our students find themselves thrust into managerial responsibilities. Not only is there knowledge to be acquired but also skills to be developed, and this can only be done through 'action' learning.

It is quite wrong for young students to be given the broad requirements of a project and then left to get on with it alone. Of course the main aim is to increase their independence and to make demands on their organising abilities. But they need support and their work needs to be monitored; this is asking no more than a manager in adult life would expect. So the tutor must make a fine judgement about how close this support and supervision should be, bearing in mind the needs of the student and the requirements of the examination board.

A typical planning tutorial might proceed through the following agenda:

- A review of progress since the last meeting

- An identification of issues and problems about which decisions need to be made in this meeting

- A discussion of each one in turn with decisions summarised

- A briefing for the next stage.

As previously, we have the problem that many projects are individual and the tutor may find that involving the whole tutorial group makes for complications. Nevertheless the advantages of the group probably outweigh the disadvantages. To make things a little easier it would always be useful to group students on the basis of their chosen topic. This might generate spin-off between the students' individual plans.

Long Term Planning

It is useful occasionally to take time off from the day to day progress in teaching and learning to look at the programme of study as a whole.

This gives the students the opportunity to raise any major issues that are giving them concern. Sometimes they may express the need to revise some critical component of the course, or to have some additional coaching in a difficult area. Sometimes they may question assumptions that have been made about their prior understanding and ask for some specific help.

Students and tutor will often find it valuable to survey the resources being used, their suitability and their availability. There may also be decisions to be made about the planning of project work, the organisation of field work, visits, etc.

Much of this might be more appropriately handled on a whole class basis, but the use of an occasional tutorial can do much to ensure that all voices, including sensitive ones, are heard.

B ## Student Responsibilities

As students gain experience in tutorials they will learn to take a more active part, making their own contributions and listening to and supporting the contributions of others. This is a good start and the tutor can build on this by encouraging them to take on greater responsibility, not only for their own work but also for the management of the tutorial.

Delegation

The main principle in all delegation is to delegate some important work, not just the unpleasant, routine chores. Students can often surprise their teachers, and even themselves, when they are given real responsibility.

Try to delegate *whole responsibilities* not just individual tasks. The student should be responsible not only for doing the work, but also for deciding how it should be done, and for reporting and being answerable at the end.

Here are some of the contributions that a student might make to the management of the tutorial:

- *Consulting* with tutor and students to determine objectives and an agenda for a tutorial, and then arranging for everyone to have a copy.

- Carrying out a *search* (in the library or elsewhere) in order to provide the group with a better resource list for a given topic.

- Keeping a *record* of decisions made at a tutorial and arranging for everyone to have a copy.

- *Maintaining* the file of tutorial records (agendas and 'minutes').

- *Corresponding* with outside organisations on behalf of the group.

- Acting as *organiser* for any occasions when the group needs to use facilities (transport, public services, etc) outside the school.

- Acting as *process observer* for a given tutorial (see below).

- Acting as *expert* to the group in a topic in which the student has particular competence and confidence.

Evaluation

Students should become involved in the evaluation of the work done during the tutorial. They should be encouraged to keep their own notes about the processes of the tutorial in order to take part in occasional discussions designed to bring about improvements. When students are trusted in this way they can make contributions which are not only sensitive and supportive, but also very constructive.

The Well-Managed Tutorial

Of course the ultimate test of a tutorial has to be expressed in terms of the educational objectives of the tutorial which we discussed in chapter 5. But it is also useful to consider the attributes of a tutorial which is effective in purely management terms. The well-managed tutorial is like a well-managed business meeting in the adult world. Here is a check list of such attributes:

- The objectives and agenda are clear and are known in advance.

- The tutorial starts on time and all quickly get down to business.

- The tutor chairs the tutorial skilfully, striking a good balance between the discipline of proceeding with the business and allowing each member to make a full and satisfying contribution.

- The students are eager to play their part. They behave as effective participants, by striking a good balance between contributing and listening, and between supporting and challenging.

- The group determines throughout to keep to the agenda.

- There is a strong tradition of recording important decisions.

- The tutorial ends satisfactorily for all concerned with a summary and a clear *contract* about all decisions and commitments.

- The small administrative matters surrounding the programme of study are dealt with briskly and efficiently.

- The students display an awareness of the communications problem, and constantly seek to clarify their own understanding and the understanding of others.

- The students are efficient in the mechanics of the system, especially with respect to deadlines for completed work.

7

Style and Techniques

Style

Techniques

STYLE AND TECHNIQUES

As part of our discussion about student skills we have stressed the distinction between knowing *about* and knowing *how*. The same is true of the skills of teaching and tutoring. Good teachers are not necessarily the most articulate in discussion about teaching, and those who can speak eloquently about it are not necessarily the best performers in the classroom. In the ideal world we would all be equally good at knowing about and at knowing how.

The problem is particularly difficult in tutoring. It is perfectly possible to have a clear vision of high standards in tutoring and to be able to describe them vividly and with conviction, but at the same time to fall well short of those standards in practice. The reasons for this are not hard to find.

- Teachers work under tremendous pressure in school. Events crowd in so fast that they rarely have an opportunity to think carefully about what they say or do. Events push them relentlessly towards directive styles.

- It is also difficult to be completely self-aware about one's own styles within a teaching situation. Generally, we tend to overestimate the amount of student participation in our own lessons.

So the twin problems of getting the *style* right and getting the *techniques* right are the major ones for the teacher who is interested in tutoring. In this chapter we attempt to analyse style and techniques, and the issues are summarised in the diagram opposite. In the final chapter we look at the implications for a staff development programme.

A Style

A teacher's style is made up of a blend of personal attributes and habitual ways of doing things. It originates in our basic philosophic stance but it is modified substantially by our experiences in school.

There are two desirable features of style in tutoring:

1) The tutor achieves a high level in the students' performance and in the students' attitudes to their work.

2) The tutor keeps a fine balance between his/her concern for their performance and concern for their sense of personal worth.

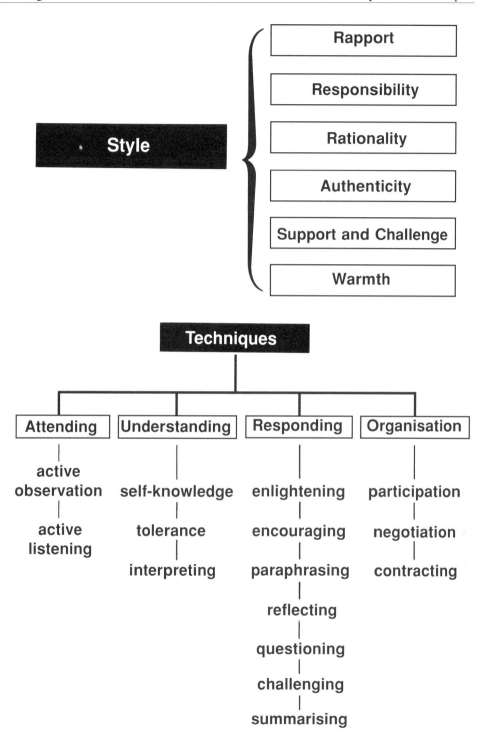

Style

- Rapport
- Responsibility
- Rationality
- Authenticity
- Support and Challenge
- Warmth

Techniques

Attending	Understanding	Responding	Organisation
active observation	self-knowledge	enlightening	participation
active listening	tolerance	encouraging	negotiation
	interpreting	paraphrasing	contracting
		reflecting	
		questioning	
		challenging	
		summarising	

Style and Techniques

This view of style can be expressed diagrammatically. The four caricatures should help to demonstrate how the variables work.

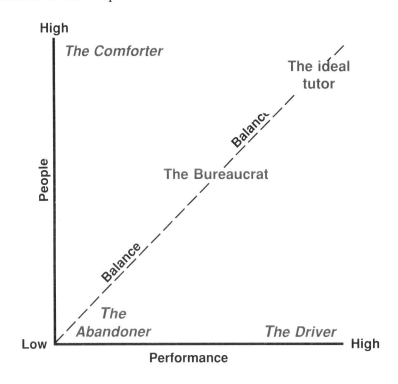

Style in Tutoring

The Abandoner	is satisfied with the minimum on all counts, and a quiet life!
The Driver	believes in hard work and discipline, rejecting 'all this human relations stuff'!
The Comforter	believes in creating a happy family and is desperate not to rock the boat by making uncomfortable demands!
The Bureaucrat	manages to keep a balance, but at the expense of overall achievement - main interest is in working to the rules.

It is surprising how easy it is to drift, almost without noticing, in the direction of one of these caricatures.

Some attempt at analysis should help us to steer a steadfast course. So what are the attributes which help in building an effective style?

Warmth

A tutor cannot have lasting influence on students unless the students feel that the tutor has a genuine concern for them. This manifests itself in all sorts of small ways, but particularly when the tutor displays interest in them as people, beyond the needs of the immediate learning task. Warmth creates confidence and trust and this leads to open and honest endeavour. The lack of it can seriously inhibit students. Of course, we must measure it carefully. There is a point beyond which it can become an objective in its own right and then might undermine the real objectives.

Rapport

Rapport is the harmonious relationship which develops within a group. The individuals are all different, yet these differences are not only respected but used in positive and constructive ways. The good tutor works hard to build up the rapport of the group. The results are good teamwork, a sense of empathy, and a strong feeling within each member of being valued. This is much more powerful than simply *hammering out agreement*, or abiding by the rule of the majority.

Responsibility

The good tutor always sets an example as a thoroughly responsible person. This involves frequently deferring to legitimate authority or to fundamental principles, and being quite explicit about it. The students should learn to expect a high degree of consistency from their tutor in this respect. Hopefully they will emulate the style.

Rationality

The tutor will always demonstrate the rational approach to decisions and action. Again the process must be explicit so that the students are able to see it happening. So it is all about explaining the reasons for decisions, thinking aloud, and being prepared to modify a decision in response to one's own deeper analysis.

Bona Fide

Being true to oneself is another attribute of a good tutor. This often means simply being straight with the learner about matters which affect him/her. It also means being honest about the role that one is playing at any given time, and being prepared to expose one's own motives and intentions. It means being prepared to admit to mistakes and being ready to discuss inadequacies in what one has to offer. There is a lot of humility in this attribute, but being true to oneself usually attracts greater respect from the students.

The Learning Climate - balance between support and challenge

Much of the style of the tutor is about balance. We have already expressed it as the balance between concern for people and concern for performance. It can also be expressed slightly differently as the balance between support and challenge. This defines the learning climate which we would like to create. Students clearly need both support and challenge. The good tutor is constantly measuring the amount of each which is being provided in an endeavour to get the balance just right.

Style is not easy to change. So much of our decision and action when faced by our students is intuitive. But we should not be defeatist. We can bring about a shift in overall style, first by being aware of the elements of which it is composed, and second by changing it piecemeal through the conscious application of techniques.

B Techniques

Techniques describe what the tutor can actually do to run a better tutorial. So they can influence the overall style and they help in the achievement of the tutorial's objectives. The approach through techniques can be very effective because techniques can be practised and observed; they represent a step-by-step way of bringing about improvement.

We are analysing techniques in four main groups: *attending* techniques, *understanding* techniques, *responding* techniques, and *organising* techniques.

Attending Techniques

The successful tutor is very alert and sensitive to individual and group attitudes and needs. There are two aspects.

Active Observation

- The tutor is aware of the importance of what the students do (sometimes as opposed to what they say) - how they arrive, where they choose to sit, how they prepare for the tutorial, how they depart.

- The tutor is conscious of body language during the tutorial and adjusts to it. The significant things are facial expressions, eye contact, and the movements of hands, arms or the whole body.

Active Listening

- The tutor gives wholehearted *attention* to what is being said by the students.

- The tutor has developed the skill of *waiting*. This may be waiting for a first contribution to be made, or while a student reflects for a short period before continuing to develop a verbal contribution.

- The tutor has developed the skill of *encouraging*. This may be achieved by a short prompt, or by a non-verbal action - a nod of the head, a raised eyebrow, a gesture of the hands.

- The tutor practises the skills of *building*. This means taking the first contributions from the students and helping them to develop them into more elaborate and meaningful statements. The tutor's contributions are kept to the absolute minimum required to achieve this. It involves the use of a number of the skills which are described later in this section.

Understanding Skills

The good tutor constantly strives to raise the level of his/her own capacity for understanding.

Self-knowledge

This is the basis of greater understanding. The tutor knows his/her own strengths and weaknesses across a broad spectrum: subject knowledge and competence, personal bias and stereotyping, and inter-personal skills. The tutor starts from a recognition that no one is perfect nor needs to be in order to conduct successful tutorials. With this self-knowledge as a base, the tutor is more likely to understand the students better.

Tolerance

Good understanding relies also on tolerance. The tutor accepts that the students are immature and probably quite ignorant. The tutor also accepts that they may not share the tutor's own styles and preferences. It is vital to join them at their starting point without rejecting or criticising. This is not to say that the tutor will necessarily agree with everything that the students say or do; it is simply affirming the need to practise tolerance. Tolerance is founded on respect.

Meaning

Finally, the good tutor will always search for the meaning behind all utterances and all actions of the students. Sometimes this can be coaxed out of them, at other times it has to be inferred. Over a period of time a tutor will claim to have got to know a group of students. This usually suggests that they are understood at the deeper level which is implied in this paragraph.

Responding Skills

Of course, the tutor must sooner or later respond. The students have an entitlement to hear what the tutor knows and thinks. It is through the responding skills that the tutor can make a big difference to the quality of students' thinking, understanding, and performance.

Enlightening

- The tutor finds opportunities to make the new knowledge more meaningful, by demonstrating its relationship to existing knowledge and its internal structure.

- The tutor provides props for the learners through the description of concrete examples, and the use of people's first hand experiences.

- The tutor helps the students to see the relevance of the new knowledge to their own lives.

Encouraging

We have already considered encouraging as a part of active listening. But the process can be developed further as a responding skill.

- The tutor provides the students with additional data or stimuli which will help them to extend and enrich their own contributions to the tutorial.

- The tutor stimulates further contribution by the use of praise and questioning.

Paraphrasing

This is a common and valuable skill in tutoring. It simply means finding different words to express the ideas of the students. This can often help them to extend an idea or to modify it slightly in order to make it more accurate or useful. The tutor is always careful to respect the student's ownership of the idea and so the student remains heavily involved.

Reflecting Feelings

This is similar to paraphrasing, but the focus is on feelings. Sometimes a student expresses a feeling about the work in preference to responding to the substance of the learning. The tutor's most helpful response is to let the student talk about it and to accept the feeling by paraphrasing it. As often as not that is the end of the matter and the work can proceed. It is generally a better strategy than trying to counteract the feeling, which is somewhat distracting. Sometimes too the expression of feeling is covering more complex thoughts which the student cannot express. A skilful tutor will often uncover those thoughts and the tutorial as a whole will benefit.

Questioning

The tutor's questions can be a powerful stimulus in the tutorial. The important principle to bear in mind is that the questions should not be conducted like a test, as though the only outcome of interest to the tutor is that a student should get the right answer. Questions should be framed so that the answer can be used in the subsequent discussion. It should be assumed that the tutor and the rest of the group are genuinely interested in the answer.

Who? What? When? Where? form the basic repertoire. It should be remembered, however, that all of these could be answered by a single word. This is equally true of the simple interrogative forms of many verbs: *Did he succeed in his mission? - Who wrote it?*

Why? and *How?* stand a better chance.

So we need to plan questions with a possible extended answer in mind. We need to encourage conjecture and more complex thought. We need to prompt the students to appreciate that there may be multiple or alternative responses. *What if...?* questions can be exciting. A challenging form of question can often help. *What possible explanations could there have been for the survival of that species?* or *What would have happened if....?*

Challenging

Wherever possible the independent work that the students undertake should be presented in challenging terms. For example, in some topics it is quite useful to point out in advance where most students make the errors or produce inadequate work, with the implication that this group of students could be the first to do otherwise! Hopefully the students will rise to the challenge.

The tutor should occasionally play the role of 'devil's advocate'. Provided students know that the tutor is adopting this role they can get considerable enjoyment and stimulus from defending an intellectual position.

Individuals can often be challenged to go beyond their own previous best performance. This challenge needs to be tailor-made and quite specific, probably focusing on a student's previous weaknesses.

But the challenge idea should be extended beyond that. If some suitable reward can be made available this can be offered in exchange for a particularly thorough piece of work involving effort beyond the normal expectation. Many teachers have personal experience of 'challenge funding' in local authority development work and will testify to the effectiveness of the technique.

Summarising

The good tutor regularly summarises and encourages the students to contribute. It is a most effective way of reinforcing learning and giving the students confidence. But it is also teaching them something about how they should organise their own studies when they do not have the support of the teacher.

Organising Skills

The Skills of Participation

All of the skills of *attending, understanding,* and *responding* will contribute towards improving the amount of the students' participation. There are some additional skills that are particularly relevant here.

a) Student Questions

Student questions are the key to their active participation. So we must create the occasions for them. Nothing inhibits student questions so much as a rapid succession of tutor's questions. The tutor believes that his/her questions are stimulating the students, and piles on the pressure. When the students appear to be flagging the tutor attempts to revive them by inviting them to ask questions. But it is too late. They have relinquished any desire to take the initiative and are now content to play a subordinate role.

So here are some specific suggestions relating to student questions:

- At the beginning invite them each to write down a question in preparation for a discussion.

- When each question is taken, respond to it positively. Repeat it. Paraphrase it. Relate it to a previous question or to the topic as a whole. Then use it as a springboard for other questions or other activity.

- Don't offer a quick answer to the question. Sustain the feeling of perplexity by paraphrasing. Increase the desire to know by challenging the other students. Through praise or warm acceptance show approval of the student's courage in asking the question.

b) **Encourage their personal involvement**

- Within the tutorial this means simply getting them to talk.

- Teach them to listen to each other and build on the contributions of the whole group.

- Encourage them to take on assignments which will support the whole group - reading, resource finding, summarising, negotiating with outside organisations.

- Encourage them to take responsible roles within the tutorial itself - chairing, recording, reporting, observing.

- Admit your own mistakes. A certain amount of fallibility can keep them alert!

- Help them to use any errors they make as starting points for profitable discussion. Praise such activity.

- Use them as evaluators. Their thoughts and feelings about the way that the programme of study is going are of immense practical value to the tutor. But using them in this way also makes them feel good about their work.

c) **Encourage more complex thought**

- Constantly press the members of the group to engage in higher levels of thought.

- Make them clarify what they are saying.

- Make them justify their assertions.

- Invite them to put forward counter proposals.

- Invite them to paraphrase what others are trying to say.

- Make them apply their knowledge in new situations.

- Invite them to ponder and to speculate.

The Skills of Negotiation

The word *negotiation* has become one of the vogue words in education. We like to think of the student engaged in serious and responsible conversation with a teacher in order to arrive at significant decisions about the choices which face the student at whatever level. Sometimes the negotiation is about long-term decisions, concerned with the choice of courses, and sometimes it is about the detail of work within a programme of study.

We still have a long way to go in negotiation. Sometimes it seems that it has been confused with the idea of letting students do as they like. But real negotiation is a sophisticated adult business. It is unreasonable to expect our students to be good performers, but there is everything to be said for regarding the tutorial as the main training ground.

Much will have to be accomplished by *example* rather than by *precept*. They need to see what skilful negotiation looks like in practice, rather than be given sets of rules to obey.

So it may be helpful to have a check list of what good negotiation looks like. Then the tutor can teach them chiefly by example with a small amount of advice when they seem ready for it.

So here are suggestions for skilled negotiation.

- The skilled negotiator spends a lot of time collecting information. This gives some breathing space, time to marshal one's thoughts, as well as illuminating the whole situation.

- The skilled negotiator is concerned about clarity, constantly trying to review and to interpret. He/she wants to make sure that any agreement really will stick.

- The skilled negotiator calms the opposite side by asking questions or making assertions in a reassuring way. This often means using a gentle overture, for example: *There's one thing that's concerning me a little ...*

- The skilled negotiator avoids value judgements which might be unwelcome. The use of insulting remarks is obviously unacceptable. But equally there is a lot to be said for avoiding saying favourable things about one's own attitudes on the grounds that this can seem 'holier than thou'.

- Above all the skilled negotiator is anxious to keep a genuine dialogue going, and so will spend a lot of time listening and will avoid the temptation of countering everything the other person says automatically.

So we need to bring our young students into the negotiation fully aware that there are several points of view present - usually the student himself/herself, the tutor, the school, the examination board, the National Curriculum, and so on. Then it is a question of trying to get a result which will satisfy all these pressures. It is not a question of winning or not winning. It is a question of finding a fair and useful solution. Being a skilled negotiator is a most satisfying role in the adult world. We should start our students at the earliest age possible.

The Skills of Contracting

It is important to bring the tutorial to a satisfactory conclusion. The students must leave with a clear vision of what has been decided. Many teachers are so convinced about this that they take the trouble to make a formal contract with the students. They may not do it in every tutorial, but whenever briefing for new tasks has been an important item on the agenda then a contract seems highly desirable.

The use of the term *contract* implies that the agreement is in writing and that the signature of student and tutor is required. Not everyone who uses the idea will wish to go that far; some will simply prefer to make a formal summary at the end.

Many enthusiasts for contracts have designed their own pro-forma. This provides headings for the student, and throughout the tutorial the tutor may prompt students to *make a note on the contract*. In this way the contract builds up naturally throughout the tutorial, and any summary at the end is simply for reinforcement.

Others prefer to let the students keep a running record of what is being decided in the tutorial - like the minutes of a meeting. But in the same way as the pro-forma the contract builds up throughout the tutorial.

The contract, however it is produced, should specify at least four things:

1) The objectives of the new learning tasks. These should state what the student will know and be able to do at the end of the task. They should also give, in outline form only, the main activities that will be necessary.

2) The resources that will be required. The guidance given in this section should be adapted to the kind of resources to be used.

  • Important core ideas in the new learning may require detailed prescription - specific paragraphs or graphics from a particular book.

- Some extensions from the core may be left much more to the individual student's discretion - general suggestions as to sources, or strategies for a library search.

3) General guidance about the organisation of the work. This will concentrate on the general approach, mentioning what is important, the possible pitfalls, the possible opportunities for extending and enriching the work.

4) The outcomes of the learning task. This should guide the student as to the nature of the finished product - its length, its style. It should also indicate the range of acceptable outcomes so that the student has choice, but within accepted limits. Finally the student should know the administrative details - the time limit for completion, and the requirements for handing in.

In building up and using contracts the tutor and students will make use of all the techniques described in this chapter. Indeed the making of the contract represents a pinnacle of achievement. It is particularly an opportunity to practise the negotiating skills described in the previous section.

The sample contract pro-forma opposite is included to help teachers design their own. The actual items and sub-items are often specific to the needs of particular subjects of the curriculum.

The contract, in essence, is a student record or profile. It is but a small step to convert this to a formative record which can become part of a full Record of Achievement. The negotiation of records of achievement is an accepted process in both schools and FE, and the skills of tutoring described in this book are exactly those needed in the pastoral situation of student and tutor.

Finally, the idea of the contracts or profile records can be extended into a much longer time-scale. Where students are engaged in courses which require substantial amounts of independent work and individual projects, they can get a stronger sense of motivation and a clearer purpose by the use of such documents.

A Model Learning Contract

NAME . . . .

FORM . . . . DATE . . . .

SUBJECT/TOPIC . . . .

. . . .

OBJECTIVES . . . .

. . . .

. . . .

. . . .

TASK DETAILS . . . .

. . . .

. . . .

RESOURCES . . . .

. . . .

. . . .

. . . .

. . . .

GENERAL NOTES . . . .

. . . .

. . . .

. . . .

. . . .

. . . .

SPECIAL AGREEMENTS AND COMMITMENTS
FOR THE TASK . . . .

. . . .

. . . .

. . . .

. . . .

NOTES ON THE OUTCOME . . . .

. . . .

. . . .

. . . .

. . . .

8

A Staff Development
Programme

A Programme of Staff Development

Peer Coaching

Conclusions

A STAFF DEVELOPMENT PROGRAMME

Tutoring deserves a sustained effort in staff development. There are two reasons for this assertion:

1) The method is so full of *potential*. Students stand to gain so much, in terms of personal development and in terms of academic achievement. Many of the broad aims of the National Curriculum, GCSE and Standard Grade cannot be realised without a marked shift in styles towards the tutorial.

2) The shift in styles and techniques which the tutorial requires are subtle and difficult to achieve without conscious effort, mutual support, and a rigorous approach to professional development.

So a staff development programme for a whole school could be based round the tutorial. It will be a broad canvas - the concerns of the tutorial touch most aspects of education. But it will not be a mere paper exercise, or a long drawn out series of discussions leading nowhere. It will be grounded in practice, focusing on what the teacher and students actually do, and what they actually say in the tutorial. At the end of it all there will be only one question to ask. Has it made a difference?

The suggestions below, summarised in the diagram opposite, are designed to help make that difference. They are set out in stages, and they will often occur in that sequential manner. But it would be unwise to adopt an inflexible programme - circumstances differ, and these suggestions should be treated as principles which should be incorporated into the institutions's own programme which has been designed according to its own needs.

A

A Programme of Staff Development

Stage 1: Awareness

- Allow the need for tutoring to emerge naturally from consideration of the implementation of the National Curriculum, NVQ, Records of Achievement and the teaching of new courses.

- Promote knowledge of the aims of the TVEI Extension and awareness of the developments which are supporting these aims. Particular reference points are:

  i)   *The General TVEI leaflet*

  ii) *Insight* - the termly TVEI Journal

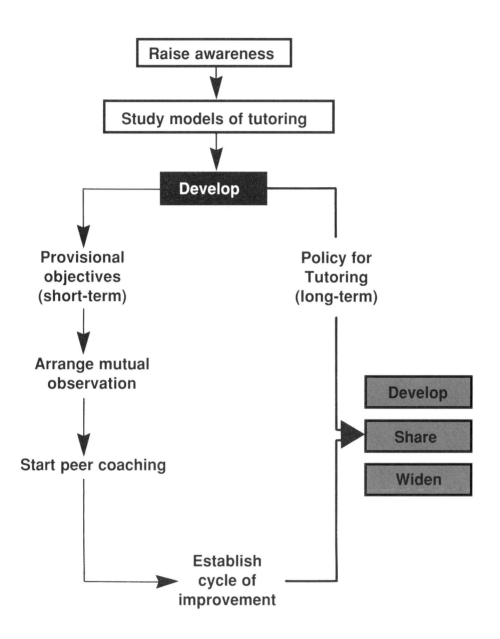

A Staff Development Programme

    iii)   *Developments in TVEI* - particularly No. 10,
           Flexible Learning.

- Encourage reading and attendance at courses. Many local authorities have appointed support teachers who specialise in Supported Self-Study, Resource-based Learning, or Flexible Learning. The TVEI Regional Project Leaders in Flexible Learning should also be contacted. These have had an unrivalled opportunity to get to know the details of developments in their regions and to be heavily involved in the setting up and running of training events. They share information across regional boundaries, and so provide a contact with a national network.

- Get commitment to the idea of a staff development programme in tutoring.

Stage 2: Observe models of tutoring

- Make contact with a school where tutorials are being developed with a view to carrying out observations. Regard these visits as a continuation of the awareness-raising process. The observation should be general in nature and not an attempt at rigorous analysis. Beware the temptations of the *spectator in the stands* syndrome! Remember that most developments in tutoring are still in their early stages. So be sympathetic and helpful.

- Use video recordings of tutorials for more detailed study. Carry out simple analyses to try to identify strengths. Again, beware the temptation only to be critical. Find the strengths and concentrate on how they could be developed. The main initiative in developing video recordings of tutorials is at present with the National Council for Educational Technology and its counterpart in Scotland, SCET. Training videos will be available early in 1991. *(Contact Julie Wright, NCET, Sir William Lyons Road, Science Park, University of Warwick, Coventry CV4 7EZ)*

Use the experiences of these early observations to generate a debate about objectives, styles, and techniques.

Stage 3: Develop objectives for tutorials

- Start work on a full-scale **'Policy For Tutoring'**. There could be discussion at whole school level and also discussion at departmental level in order to handle matters specific to each subject.

- Regard the Policy For Tutoring as a long term project. Don't let the fact that it is not finished hold up development work.

- Prepare some *provisional* objectives to guide any immediate developments that are planned. For example, a department may decide to start some tutorial activity with some particular improvements in mind. These should be set out as limited short-term objectives.

Use this book as a source of ideas for objectives. It has been written in a structured way in order to make this possible. Develop the Policy on similar lines. An example of this approach is described in detail in the handbook *Classroom Management*, Book 2 in this series.

Stage 4: Set up a system of mutual support

- Make some explicit arrangements for mutual observation. This is not easy! Possible ways forward are:

    1) Make small timetable arrangements to enable a pair of teachers to observe each other.

    2) Use supply teachers to cover during staff development time.

    3) Use the services of an advisory teacher who is supporting the development to give the necessary flexibility.

    4) Encourage departments to exploit the flexibility that they may have as a result of some form of block timetabling.

    5) Encourage mutual support between departments where the interest in tutoring is strong.

- Regard the existence of a mutual observation system as an opportunity to develop the idea of **Peer Coaching.**

B Peer Coaching

The Cycle of Improvement

The main characteristic of this system is its cyclical nature. The diagram overleaf illustrates this.

It is important that for the purposes of this work the partners should regard themselves as equals. It would be unhelpful if a senior person were to adopt the role of observer as part of the exercise of supervision of the work of colleagues.

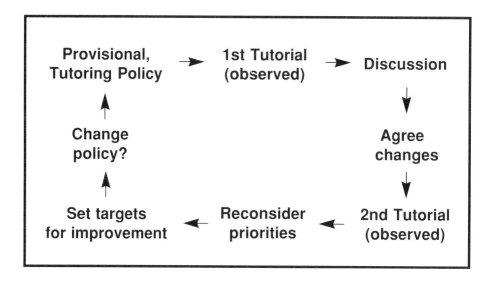

The Improvement of Tutoring

Each 'tour' through the cycle starts with a planning session at which priorities are agreed. The main question is: what difference are we trying to make in the conduct of the tutorial?

During observation the observer makes notes or works to an agreed observation schedule, but does not take part in any way.

As soon as possible after the tutorial the teachers discuss the tutorial. They try to reach agreement about their conclusions, and then make plans for the next tutorial.

The purpose of the cycle approach is to develop improvements on a cumulative basis. Each tutorial is seen as the base line for the improvements in the next.

There are two ways of organising the roles of observer and observed. Both seem to work well.

1) One teacher becomes the observer for a whole sequence of tutorials and all efforts are concentrated on the coaching of this teacher. Then the roles are reversed.

2) Both teachers are tutoring, observing and being observed. The two sequences are running in parallel. This provides more raw material for discussion.

The Role of the Observer

It is important that the observer does not adopt a superior judgemental stance. The observer is there simply to observe and to make the observations available to the teacher. It is best in the early stages to stick to a limited number of modest objectives and to adopt procedures which clearly identify the teacher, not the observer, as the leader. When confidence grows, of course, the objectives can be much more challenging and the debate can become much freer. Even then it is better if the initiative is retained by the teacher.

The Development of Peer Coaching

The Early Stages

In the early stages the objectives are modest and the observer carefully defers to the teacher, making sure that reports and feedback are detached. This helps build confidence and a feeling of mutual trust. Many of the simpler techniques of tutoring can be improved through this mechanism.

The Later Stages

As confidence grows, however, both partners in the enterprise will become aware of the need for debate of a much more analytical nature. Tutoring is not just about applying some simple techniques. It is much more complex, concerned with the design of a whole learning experience. The observations will now begin to range widely:

- The purposes of the tutorial
- The agenda
- The intellectual and attitudinal objectives which are being pursued
- The style and techniques of the tutor
- The performance of the students in terms of participating and negotiating skills.

For any given tutorial it will be essential to have a small set of objectives as the main purpose of the observation. But it should now be possible to allow the observer to make contributions from any standpoint.

Widening the Scope

Teachers who are engaged in the kind of debate described in the last section will find it frustrating if they are not able to share their experiences and thinking with a wider audience.

How far this can be extended must be a matter for local decision. Clearly it is helpful if the whole school is involved and a **Policy for Tutoring** is high on the agenda. Sometimes, TVEI *clusters* of schools and colleges have been established in order to share ideas about techniques, to share materials, and to engage in some joint planning of schemes of work. This is professionalism of a very high order and it offers great promise.

C

Conclusions

Tutoring, as described in this book, is not simple or easy. It is ambitious, but not unrealistically so. It can afford to be ambitious because as soon as the management problems have been overcome the potential for *making a difference* is very great. Within the tutorial experience students stand a chance of becoming, in the words of Carl Rogers, *Fully Functioning Persons.*

In this final chapter we have explored how teachers may prepare themselves through sharing and through mutual support. When teachers work together in this way they are not only giving their students a preparation for life, they are also realising their own professional vision.

APPENDIX   A Selected List of References

Bailey, D. (1987) *Guidance in Open Learning: A Manual of Practice.* NICEC.

Brighouse, T. (1991) *What Makes a Good School?* Network Educational Press.

Dillon, J. (1988) *Questioning and Teaching.* Croom Helm.

Goodlad, S and Hirst, B. (1989) *Peer Tutoring.* Kogan Page.

Holt, J. (1981) *Teach Your Own.* Lighthouse Press.

Inskipp, F. (1986) *Counselling: The Trainer's Handbook.* NEC.

Lewis, R. (1986) *The Schools Guide to Open Learning.* NEC.

Markless, S and Lincoln, P. (1989) *Tools for Learning: Information Skills and Learning to Learn in Secondary Schools.* NFER.

Miller, J. (1982) *Tutoring: the Guidance and Counselling Role of the Tutor in Vocational Preparation.* Longmans for FEU.

NEC/NCET. (1989) *Implementing Flexible Learning: A Resource Pack for Trainers.*

Powell, R. (1991) *Resources for Flexible Learning.* Network Educational Press.

Rogers, C. (1983) *Freedom to Learn in the Eighties.* Merrill.

Training & Enterprise Education Directorate   *TVEI Developments 10: Flexible Learning.*

Waterhouse, P. (1988) *Supported Self-Study: An Introduction for Teachers.* NCET.

Waterhouse, P. (1990) *Classroom Management.* Network Educational Press.

Waterhouse, P. (1990) *Flexible Learning: An Outline.* Network Educational Press.

Whittrock, M. (1986) *Handbook of Research on Teaching.* Macmillan.

INDEX

The Teaching and Learning Series

This book, *Tutoring* is the fourth in the series and is closely related to four others which examine important issues both for the classroom teacher and the school or college manager.

Book 1, *Flexible learning: an Outline*, by **Philip Waterhouse** provides an outline of all the key questions in the debate on teaching and learning styles. He examines the rationale, contexts and methods of flexible learning:

- The National Curriculum
- Tutoring
- Assessment
- The flexible use of space, time, money and people
- TVEI
- The use of libraries and resource centres
- Records of Achievement
- Study skills.

Flexible Learning: an Outline is a **handbook**. Each chapter provides an agenda, a checklist of key issues and will be invaluable to all those interested in stimulating discussion or raising awareness on the subject of how teachers teach and how students learn.

ISBN 1 85539 003 5 £6.50

Book 2, *Classroom Management,* by **Philip Waterhouse**, provides a detailed insight into the management of a wide variety of teaching and learning strategies. It provides practical advice on:

- Planning and organisation of schemes of work
- Differentiation
- Assignments
- Management of resources
- The organisation and layout of classrooms
- Assessment and recording
- Managing whole-class, small-group and individual work.

The book will be a valuable handbook for both classroom teachers and those managing teaching and learning in schools and colleges.

ISBN 1 85539 004 3 £6.50

Book 3, *Resources for Flexible Learning*, by **Robert Powell**, provides practical advice on the complex question of resources.

- Defining flexible resources
- Choosing and evaluating resources
- Adapting existing materials for differentiation
- Making full use of libraries/resource centres
- Preparing study guides
- Thinking about design and layout
- Using desktop publishing.

The book will suggest ways in which teachers and students can use a wide variety of resources both to satisfy the demands of the National Curriculum and to develop independent learning skills.

ISBN 1 85539 005 1 £6.50

Book 5, *What Makes a Good School?* by **Tim Brighouse** identifies those features of school organisation and management which are essential elements of successful teaching and learning. It examines:

- Leadership in the successful school
- Environment in the successful school
- Staff development in the successful school
- Collective review in the successful school
- The organisation of learning in the successful school
- Successful teaching and learning.

ISBN 1 85539 007 8 £6.50

This book is an introduction to a major series by Tim Brighouse (Research Machines Professor of Education, University of Keele) which explores each of the topics above in some depth. This series will be published by Network Educational Press Ltd.

Book 6, *Flexible Learning: Evidence Examined*, by **Mike Hughes** documents a four-year case study of flexible learning approaches.

Mike Hughes used flexible learning with all his classes 11-16 whilst colleagues in his department continued to teach the same curriculum more formally to classes of similar ability. The book presents the results produced by the different approaches:

- Examination results
- Attitudes of pupils
- Test scores
- Perceptions of parents
- Motivation and behaviour
- Views of 6th Form Teachers

The evidence is factual. The results are stunning. Readers can draw their own conclusions.

ISBN 1 85539 013 2 £8.50

Other Publications from Network Educational Press

Education: Putting the Record Straight

Education has been under attack for some time; from newspapers and politicians. Headlines such as "standards falling", "progressive methods blamed", "educational mafia" are commonplace.

In this book 16 respected figures from the world of education put the record straight . The contributors include: **Eric Bolton,** fromer chief HMI, **Duncan Graham,** former Chief Executive of the National Curriculum Council, **Brian Cox,** former chairman of the English working group, **Paul Black,** former chairman of the Task Group on Assessment and Testing, **Joan Sallis,** President of the Campaign for the Advancement of State Education, and **Ted Wragg,** Professor of Education at Exeter University.

The authors present a more accurate and positive account of education than is currently fashionable amongst politicians. Indeed, all four Headteacher Association from both the state and independent sector have recommended it as **"essential reading for teachers, governors and all who care about our schools".**

ISBN 1 85539 011 6 £7.50 (includes p+p)

Basics for School Governors, by Joan Sallis.

School governors are overwhelmed with instructions on **what** they have to do. This book is different. It concentrates on helping them to do it.

Roles
- How and why schools came to have governors
- The different types of school and their governing bodies
- Governors' role... drawing the line... decision-making
- Governors as representatives

Relationships
- ... with the headteacher
- ... with teachers
- ... with the LEA

Rules and Good Practices
- working in unity... trust... loyalty... equality
- Better meetings... the ground rules
- Getting involved in the school
- Improving teamwork, including chairing skills.

This book will appeal to headteachers, chairs of governing bodies and to governors.

Joan Sallis is nationally known and respected for her writing and lecturing on school government and her weekly advice column in the Times Educational Supplement. Above all, she is known for treating difficult issues with humanity and humour and in everyday language.

She believes passionately that a better partnership between schools and their users offers the only hope for well funded and respected state education.

ISBN 1 85539 012 4 £6.50 (includes p+p)

Study Guides from Network Educational Press

Study Guides support the development of high quality independent skills, project work, group work, core skills and cross-curricular themes.

Each Network Educational Press guide sets out in student friendly language:

- key learning objectives
- a resources section with ideas on where information can be found
- guidance on how students might plan and organise the work/enquiry
- key ideas, concepts or skills to be covered
- hints on ways in which students might present their findings
- a structure which links easily with records of achievement.

Each guide is photocopiable and allows students and teachers to record additional information - personal targets, assessment criteria, deadlines, length, etc.

Study guides are currently available in :

Key Stage 3	History
Key Stage 4	Geography, Business Studies, Humanities, English Literature, English Language
A Level	English Literature, History

Available Summer Term 1993

Key Stage 3	Science
Key Stage 4	Science

Available during Autumn 1993

Key Stages 3/4	Technology, Modern Languages
A Level	Geography, Physics, Chemistry, Biology, Economics, Business Studies, Sociology, Communications/Media, Psychology
GNVQ/NVQ	Business, Art and Design, Health and Social Care, Hotel and Catering, Travel, Tourism and Leisure, Hairdressing and Beauty

Network Educational Press Publications

For further details of Network Educational Press publications please write to:

Network Educational Press
PO Box 635
STAFFORD
ST17 OJR

Telephone: 0785 225515
Fax: 0785 228566